NEW FRONTIERS

NEW
FRONTIERS

by HENRY A. WALLACE

Whitworth College
Spokane, Wn.

REYNAL & HITCHCOCK

New York

CONTENTS

v

10,014

CONTENTS

Fourth Section
UNTROD PATHS

FIRST SECTION

BETWEEN TWO WORLDS

CHAPTER
I

EXPLORERS AND PIONEERS

THE United States is like a boy eighteen years old, possessed of excellent health and a strong body, but so unsettled in his mind and feelings that he doesn't know what to do next.

In the old days before the World War our fathers and grandfathers had their troubles and disagreements, but they agreed for the most part that this was a land of unlimited opportunity; that we would have continually more machinery and more inventions; that our cities would be getting bigger, our land values higher, and our opportunities for personal profit greater all the time.

For ten generations white people on this continent moved forward in this faith. There were times of serious setback, for example, the thirties, seventies, and nineties of the last century, but in those days depression could be cured by the pioneer virtue of optimistic grab and toil. Continual immigration from abroad, expansion into the new lands of the West and the building of railroads and highways acted as feeders to growing cities. These developments confirmed in our fathers those energetic individualistic traits which are peculiarly American. "Be up and coming. Work hard. Look out for yourself. Fear God and take your own part. Let's go. Up and at 'em." Every red-blooded American responds to such phrases even today.

In four generations our ancestors did most of the work of cutting the trees, draining the fields, and all the varied building of houses, barns, highways, railroads, skyscrapers and factories. Feverishly they worked, carrying out the injunction of the old hymn, "Work for the night is coming when man works no more."

It is easy for those of us who now are twenty-five years of age, and who in spite of earnest search have been unable to find a job, to feel scornful of the mess these older Americans made of things. In a way the feeling is justified; but before despising our first pioneers, it seems to me that youth today should appreciate the terrific labors needed to bring a continent so rapidly under physical control. Whether our fathers planned or managed or invented or worked with their hands, they really did something. Wherever we look we are impressed with their handiwork.

Present-day youth is in debt to these pioneers, just as they, in their turn went in debt to a still older generation in the older settled regions of the earth. Pioneers generally pay high interest rates and borrow too much money. One of the reasons they are able to do so much work is that they bring in from outside tremendous quantities of money and labor. They keep the men and pay back the money by sending out the extra stuff they are able to produce. In a thinly settled community, man-labor produces more than pioneers can consume, so they ship out the surplus to pay their debts.

The tragic joke on the United States is that we went

to bed as a pioneer debtor nation in 1914 and woke up after a nightmare of world madness as a presumably mature creditor nation in 1920. We were full grown in the same sense that a boy of eighteen is full grown. But ever since 1920 that boy of eighteen has been playing in the sand pile.

We educated our children—among them, millions of unemployed young—in the belief that the United States was still a pioneer country where the rugged, individualistic virtues of hard work and saving would inevitably bring success. We did not tell our sons and daughters that they were caught between two worlds, and that in the new world it will take more than hard work and saving to insure salvation.

I look at the unemployed, especially the younger ones among them, and am reminded of the verse from the Psalms: "The stone which the builders rejected has become the head of the corner." In all truth, one of the most significant facts of this age is the continuous unemployment of millions of good people. Out of this is bound to come pressure which will either destroy the old world, or create a new world, or do both.

Impatient youth, misguided, has furnished the spearhead for many of the strong-arm movements in Europe. Their inexperience, and their justifiable resentment against the situation they have inherited can be easily played upon. In this country, Yale graduates are actually working at jobs which pay $12 a week. The mother of a friend of mine recently advertised for a housemaid; she received thirty applications for the job, and twenty-five of these were girls who had graduated from college. Beyond all this, there are the thousands whom college has not, perhaps, trained to think patiently and objectively, and who can get no jobs at all. It is entirely possible that unless they can be shown there are possibilities of honest and thrilling work for them, in reshaping this democracy, they will join hands with other disgruntled groups of debtors and unemployed, and take us much faster to the left or right than we middle-aged, middle-course people want to go. They can help hurry us into such economic and social nightmares as now afflict certain older countries, with ignorant, somewhat militaristic youth movements out in front.

More immediately, there is a peril to freedom in the possibility of these young unemployed forming a lobby with other abused or aggrieved groups, and pushing, as have the veterans of past wars, for a continuing dole or lifetime pension. Quite seriously, there is danger of such drives from people who might be called, as time goes on, wounded veterans of the depression; and mere talk will not meet this danger. It is plainly the duty of the Government to see, by devices however bold and unprecedented, that jobs are made available for these people before they become psychologically disabled.

The people of my generation, those born from 1880 to 1895, can see and feel the inevitable pressure. We want to see the new world safely born, but we do not want the old world destroyed. The new world must be born from the body of the old world; for if the old is destroyed prematurely the new will also die and chaos will ensue.

My generation must face both ways.

It is our privilege and disadvantage to look at the Bourbons, the wealthy troglodytes of the preceding generation, repeating in their ignorance outworn phrases, seeking to patch their outworn economic structure and defend it from the poverty-stricken radicals, many of whom are just as ignorant as the troglodytes.

My generation wishes the new generation would spend more time trying to build seaworthy vessels in which to reach a new world and less time bothering with the troglodytes, who are rapidly dying off, anyway.

All of us under sixty years of age are desperately in need of some means of conveyance to this new world. Few past the age of fifty like to think of building such vessels. That is left for youth. I think the youth of America is about ready to try it. And there are some gray-heads among them. It will be a journey toward frontiers quite different from any we have ever known in the United States.

Our young people may wait until we are ready for them to begin, or they may not; but they will not wait forever. During the past four jobless years they have become terribly disillusioned. They are poor in experience, influence, learning, and money. Doubtless they need to know much more than they do about the facts of today. Most of all, they need to have their imaginations aroused to the possibilities of the future.

The younger people of the United States have more marvelous things to work with during the next generation than any people ever had. We have in the United States, extraordinary resources of rich soil and abundant coal, with petroleum and minerals conveniently located. Our proportion of resources to population is very great. With ordinary common sense a high standard of living in terms of material things is almost inevitable. Our climate is invigorating to human beings. The human beings now here have been drawn from among the most intelligent and vigorous racial stocks of the old world. Railways, high-ways, factories, and all the varied equipment necessary for abundant production and rapid distribution have been built. Able research men are at work in the endowed insti-tutions, the State experiment stations, in the Federal Gov-ernment and in the commercial laboratories, finding new and better ways of getting things done.

Able men, unequalled resources, inventive genius—here are the materials which the older generation, partly as a result of inept leadership, partly as a result of war, have so terribly foozled. Here is the challenge to all younger adaptable spirits possessing sufficient courage and insight to enter upon a plan of national coordination, realistic, yet idealistic.

Columbus did not know he had discovered a new world in 1492. His discovery did not make much difference to the old world for twenty or thirty years. But from 1530 onward the new world became more and more a dominat-ing fact in old world activities.

To discover and conquer North and South America took millions of explorers and pioneers of many types, classes and races. Most of them were misfits in the old world. They were poor; they held strange religious beliefs; they did not want to submit to military service: in many ways, they dissented.

A few were criminals. But all were adventurous and desirous of building new life in a new world. Think of that long procession of explorers followed by the pioneers and the builders—all kinds of people inflamed with a deep desire to conquer the resources they saw spread out before them.

Of all such men the most significant, in my opinion, were Washington, Jefferson, and Lincoln. Here were not only builders in the new world which Columbus discovered, but prophets of a new world worthy of that name, a world wherein diversity will be maintained without sacrificing unity.

"The New World": at a time of tremendous pressure and distress, that phrase rang through Europe to lift the hearts of the defeated, restless and dissatisfied. It aroused hope of romantic adventure and of sudden riches in gold and furs. But those who came to settle here found that pioneering must be paid for in sweat, blood and strange diseases, in the suffering of long, slow toil.

They paid that price, and the heritage they leave us is rather bitter—a rich land racked and mismanaged, with huge accumulations of goods and wealth, yet with millions of our people deprived and helpless. Today we again have a situation like that in Europe three hundred or four hundred years ago. In some ways I believe it is far more significant. We have millions of people with good bodies and minds who can't get jobs. They are just as good people as those who left Europe for America three hundred years ago. They are looking for another new world.

Physically there is none. No more free land worth having is to be had for the taking. But we can work over what we have of the earth's surface, and what we have of human potentialities for achieving true civilization, stability and peace. We can have our new world, if we have it in us and if we are willing to pay the price.

This new world I am talking about cannot be found on the maps. The new frontiersmen need not cross the ocean. Some people call it a state of mind. To enter it calls for an adventurous spirit, clean hearts and staying-power.

All of us, even the old folks who believe that they can make big profits again in the good old-fashioned way long for this land of tomorrow. Nobody really likes things as they are. But it will take more than vague good-will and reminiscent hopes to get us to something better. The vessels we need now must be sturdily built of mind-stuff, and they will not be seaworthy until by common consent we agree that they are safe. I have been out on several exploring expeditions aboard new inventions of social conveyance as crude and experimental as Robert Fulton's steamboat. In succeeding chapters I will tell some of the things I have learned.

This vague new world has thus far been approached chiefly by restless, romantic men who feel that the vast riches of a cooperative good life can be attained suddenly by making a speech on the New Deal, by electing some one to Congress, by writing a book, or by passing a law. All these things may be a part of the necessary pioneering but the work that finally counts will be slower, less romantic and infinitely more difficult.

Our land of tomorrow must be surveyed, and trails hacked out. To go in and take possession means mental and spiritual toil, comparable with the physical toil of those who built the New England stone fences, cleared the Ohio woods, drained northern Iowa and built the great highways of the past and present. Speech makers and enthusiasts prepared the way for all such definite jobs but the actual doing was in the hands of men with a rare capacity for planning. They had no romantic illusions; they knew the cost and decided to pay it. Hearts, minds and wills were set to the accomplishment of definite physical tasks, and the jobs were done with a rather remarkable continuous joy in the accomplishment, even though women folks and the children were often offered up as tragic sacrifices.

What we approach is not a new continent but a new state of heart and mind resulting in new standards of accomplishment. We must invent, build and put to work new social machinery. This machinery will carry out the Sermon on the Mount as well as the present social machinery carries out and intensifies the law of the jungle.

Thus we who live in the land of yesterday exhort each other with high sounding phrases to go pioneering anew. That is all right, but it should also be stated that the hard, daily work in this land of tomorrow will be appalling, and it will not lighten until vast but possible changes have been brought about in human hearts and minds.

The greatest hope is that hearts and minds will be changed in a considerable measure by the changed nature of the work. The work will be literally of a million different kinds; and it will move increasingly to an enforced realization that unrestrained selfishness is ruinous to everyone.

The plan cannot be sketched out definitely in advance any more than William Penn could sketch out for the next

100 years the destiny of Pennsylvania. This does not mean that the central core of a plan will not begin to emerge, or that the smaller segments should not be definitely blue-printed. But it does suggest that there must be a combination of flexibility and determination in definite execution.

If the people of the United States are to move definitely and determinedly into the land of a cooperative good life, we must examine all of our institutions, traditions, and habits of mind without fear or prejudice, and see to what extent changes should be made. This job is as ceaseless and as factually detailed as that of carrying the old frontier to the Pacific Coast.

To illustrate the complications of building a balanced social machinery to fit a suddenly changed situation, I describe in some detail in the third section of this book the farm troubles since 1920 and the way we undertook to meet them in 1933 and 1934 under the Agricultural Adjustment Act. The story sounds as complicated as the invention of the modern automobile, but I am convinced it is just as important. To a social inventor definite human responses to new rules of the game, in American commerce and agriculture, are as important as were the existing laws of physics and mechanics to the first automotive inventors.

I hope nobody will get the idea in reading this book that I have it in for the rich people. Most of them are just as mixed-up and well-meaning as any one else. They are not intentionally harmful. But it happens that many of these rich people have extraordinary powers over the social structure, and they have not learned to exercise these powers in the social interest, because past rules of the game for big and little have laid emphasis on getting money and power rather than on working for something larger and more permanent.

Many rich people and their children are anxious to lead the way toward a better state; but their knowledge of facts has naturally been limited because of the way in which they have been brought up. Millions of children of would-be American millionaires are not very different. Many of our farm and labor leaders cling as strongly to the land of yesterday as our richest people do.

Those who cross new frontiers in this country will of necessity insist that we approach the problems of any one region or class without being small about it. How does the solution of this local or class question affect the total welfare? This question must be raised again and again not merely as sentimental lip-service to the cause of national unity or world unity; but in response to a mathematical realization that in a world such as ours, short-time, local, selfish solutions merely create confusion and lead to ultimate economic disaster.

Those who join in this resettlement must be steadily resolute and tough-minded. Otherwise they will be as disappointed as the gentlemanly gold hunters of Captain John Smith's Jamestown expedition. It is a real land we are bound for, but successful living in it will demand even greater tension of spirit, and on a far broader scale, than was demanded of the Pilgrim Fathers.

CHAPTER
II

NEW RULES

TWO aspects of the problem stand out clearly. One has to do with planning in the physical sense of the term. The other has to do with changing the rules of the game—with laws governing tariffs, money, the regulation of corporations, taxation, and railroad and public utility rates.

We must control that part of our individualism which produces anarchy and widespread misery. If the majority of us are to have automobiles, we must obey the traffic lights and observe certain rules of common decency in order to get speedily and safely from one place to another. In the process our individuality has been curbed, but once certain habits of mutual consideration are established, we discover that the advantages outweigh the handicaps. The range of individual expression has really been widened.

Insofar as the process of production and distribution operates on a large scale over wide territories, it will be absolutely necessary for the state to assume its true functions of "directing, watching, stimulating and restraining as circumstances suggest or necessity demands." The words quoted are from no less a radical than Pope Pius XI, who has also stated that there should be "a reasonable

15

Whitworth College
Spokane, Wn.

relationship between the prices obtained for the products of the various economic groups, agrarian, industrial, etc." Most broadminded people will further agree that it is a function of the state to promulgate such a spirit of justice as will bring about that harmonious proportion in which "men's various economic activities combine and unite into one single organism and become members of a common body, lending each other mutual help and services."

Obviously, certain limits must be placed on competition and individualism. These limits should be placed by a state in the justice of whose acts there is absolute confidence. The limits should not deal with irritating particulars but with broad outlines. On these broad outlines, there should be substantial unanimity of opinion among thinking people in both the Republican and Democratic parties, and among leaders of labor, industry and agriculture. If such agreement can be reached there will be infinite opportunities for the 125 million individuals of the United States to develop their ruggedness to mutual advantage instead of to their competitive disadvantage.

It is important for all, and for younger people especially, to realize that the New Deal spirit ebbs and flows. Ordinarily, the progressive liberals get a real opportunity to change the rules only about once in a generation. Human nature is such that complacency prevails and conservatives stay in the saddle until things get pretty bad. From a logical point of view the leadership of the United States from 1920 to 1930 was bad. But the conservatives stayed in power. Most people resolutely refuse to think politically if they have jobs, a place to sleep and something to eat and wear. The economic well-being of the moment was pumped up by a false statesmanship. It took ten years and an economic smash before the people would heed the warnings of those who said, "This thing is built on sand."

Most of the so-called young liberals of today received their first political inspiration between 1906 and 1915 from Woodrow Wilson and Theodore Roosevelt. They saw liberalism go out of date in the '20's and wondered if the American people had permanently accepted a Belly-God. The young men who today are between eighteen and thirty years of age and who are anxious to see America built over fundamentally and completely in line with their dreams, will perhaps also have an opportunity to watch the conservatives get back into power. This may not come for eight, twelve or sixteen years, but it will come almost as surely as prosperity returns. People like to be comfortable and "let alone." The conservative is bound to triumph fully half the time.

But it must also be remembered that there is something inherently inadequate and often rotting about comfort. The conservative type of mind is constitutionally incapable of understanding the inevitability of certain changes. A story told me recently by the president of a large corporation illustrates the point. As a young man he worked in one of the first automobile shops in the country, in Washington. Employed as a mechanic, he was permitted also to act as salesman. He sold cars to many wealthy people in Washington. Having made a record in sales he was sent to New York and then to Detroit, which had not yet seen the beginning of its automobile business. A conservative friend warned him that the automobile was a plaything of the rich, and that work in the automotive field offered no future. The young salesman, at heart and in his future works a liberal, at length responded to the urgings of his conservative friend and abandoned the automobile business at the very time of its promise. Oddly, his conservative swing away from motor cars carried him into selling Twenty-Mule-Team Borax.

As a rule the conservative type of mind is so instinctively and continuously self-centered that it is always being surprised by changing forces. The liberals need the conservatives and the conservatives need the liberals. Only by forthright attack and counter-attack can the people be stimulated really to think.

I am not suggesting that all our younger people be liberals. There are many who should be conservatives. I am deeply concerned, however, that the leadership of the future, whether liberal or conservative, should grapple more definitely and clearly with the facts and forces involved. It seems a pity that the liberals and conservatives, the Democrats and the Republicans, as we call them now, should spend so much time calling each other names. There are tremendously important problems to be put before the people. It may not be good politics to conduct this education, but it is absolutely vital if our democracy is to survive.

CHAPTER
III

MIDDLE COURSES

I AM hoping we can advance by means of an aroused, educated Democracy. Socialism, Communism, and Fascism, it is true, have the advantage of certain precise rules not available to Democracy. They make the path to the land of tomorrow seem straight and short. The only rules a democracy can rely upon make the path seem by comparison long and tortuous. But the point is that most Americans think less rigid rules and the clash of free opinion allowed by Democracy will in the long run take us farther than will the precise, decisive dogma of Communism or Fascism. So do I.

There is nothing novel or sensational about the rules of the game I have in mind. Until recently, however, the full significance of such rules has been obscured, and the rules have been manipulated more or less secretly for the benefit of the few at the expense of the many. Now the time seems ripe for a change in behalf of the many.

The first step is to understand these rules in all their significance. They have to do with such devices as the tariff, the balance of international payments, monetary policy, subsidies, taxation, price and production policies, and railroad rate regulations. Their significance lies in the fact that by their manipulation it is possible to direct, stimulate, restrain, and balance those forces which have to do with proportioning the national income. All governments that have advanced beyond the pioneer stage find it necessary to use such controls, in lieu of free competition. In using them, a democracy worthy of the name must be guided by concern for social justice and social charity—in other words, the greatest good for the greatest number.

Reliance upon such devices to redistribute income and opportunity, is not the way of Socialism, of Communism or of Fascism. Neither is it the way of the free-booter capitalists of the neo-Manchester school of economics. With their devotion to unlimited competition, these people seem to think the traffic lights should be removed so motorists and pedestrians might illustrate the doctrine of the survival of the fittest at every street corner. It is necessary in a democracy to furnish the red and green lights to guide the traffic, but not to supply drivers for every car on the road.

Long before the World War, competition was limited by rules, both public and private. Since then, it has been limited increasingly. The vital question is: In whose behalf is competition limited? Is the limitation making the rich richer and the poor poorer? If so, there is danger that a day may come when the extreme left will join hands with the extreme right to bring about that most dangerous of all forms of government, a corrupt oligarchy, maintaining itself in power by pandering to the vices and prejudices of a bitter, materialistic, perennially unemployed multitude.

An enduring democracy can be had only by promoting a balance among all our major producing groups, and in such a way as does not build up a small, inordinately wealthy class. The danger in democracies, as we have known them in the past, is this: All too easily, under pressure of changing conditions, they play into the hands of either the extreme left or the extreme right. The same legislators will allow themselves to be stampeded by scared capitalists toward the extreme right, and by the unemployed toward the extreme left. The complexities and the confusion of modern civilization are such that legislators quickly forget objectives of social and economic balance, and give way to the special pressures of the moment.

There is no likelihood of a dictatorship in this country, whether of the proletariat, of the technicians, or of the financiers, unless our middle class is wiped out. If we get into a really big war, the after-effect might include something of this sort; but without such a catastrophe it would seem that we have much better than an even chance to use our democratic powers and escape such regimentation by government as has been invoked in the totalitarian or autarchic states of Europe.

There is something wooden and inhuman about the government interfering in a definite, precise way with the details of our private and business lives. It suggests a time of war with generals and captains telling every individual exactly what he must do each day and hour. The Great War gave blueprint planning and regimented adherence to a plan a tremendous impetus. For several years hundreds of millions of people had definite objectives held before them in a tone of command. Their psychology was to some extent definitely altered. With their middle classes pauper-ized, and with the war methods of planning as an inspira-tion, it is small wonder that Italy, Germany, and Russia have since continued blueprint planning.

I see no reason as yet why we in the United States should go into precise detailed planning except, perhaps, with respect to natural resources and to certain rather small segments of our national life on an emergency basis. With the situation that exists and is likely to exist in the United States for the next ten years, the chief objective of our democracy should be so to manage the tariff, and the money system, to control railroad interest rates; and to encourage price and production policies that will main-tain a continually balanced relationship between the income of agriculture, labor, and industry.

I know how difficult this will be. Because of the exceed-ingly fluid nature of world events it is impossible to say; "We are going to depend altogether for the restoration of this harmonious relationship by refraining at once and completely from producing the products which formerly we have sold abroad." As a matter of fact, it is impossible to make any absolutely definite statement, aside from a declaration that these powers must be used in such propor-tion that they will add up to make sense.

After the War and until March of 1933, these powers were used in such proportions that they made apparent sense only. This apparent sense was attained only because large sums of United States money were loaned abroad year after year until 1930. After 1930 and until 1933, the customary proportions of these powers did not add up to make sense, and we therefore had misery. Since March

1933, we have had some slight surcease of misery because governmental action with respect to gold increased the purchasing power of foreign currencies for the American dollar, and brought about, for the time being, a more harmonious relationship between the export agriculture of the United States and the rest of the nation. This was an appropriate move and in the right direction, because the exporting agricultural regions of the United States had suffered more than any other part of the nation. This was not blueprint planning. It was merely taking a temporary step to remedy a critical maladjustment.

The greatest need of a modern democracy is to understand how completely and mathematically moral is the running of a modern state. This has to do especially with the internal budget and the external balance sheet with other nations. From 1920 to 1930 a fictitious prosperity was purchased for the United States. The administrations in power unconcernedly permitted large loans abroad at the same time that tariffs were increased. The false market built up for our export products during this period gave us an apparent urban prosperity from 1922 to 1929, but when the bubble finally burst, there was a loss of wealth mounting into the tens of billions of dollars. That loss came because the leaders of American thought and action were unable to think in terms of ordinary double-entry arithmetic as applied to the international balance between the United States and other nations.

It is just as necessary to think clearly and honestly about the domestic national budget. In times of war or great depression, the Treasury must go overboard at the rate of hundreds of millions of dollars annually. This cannot go on indefinitely. The time comes when the outgo must be cut down or the income of the Treasury must be increased. Otherwise there is a deficit. For a period of several years the deficit may be successfully paid in bonds. Then it must be paid in paper money. This is usually the prelude to uncontrolled inflation. Conceivably, paper money might be used to prevent uncontrolled inflation, but no one has yet explained how.

The early stages of uncontrolled inflation usually result in farm prosperity and great hardship for the upper half of the middle class in the cities. When uncontrolled inflation comes to an end, the middle class is almost wholly wiped out and the farmers are in terrible trouble. Almost invariably, they find it difficult in time of inflation to pay off their mortgages in inflated money and at the same time avoid the contracting of new debts.

The budget deficit of the last year of the Hoover Administration and the first year of the Democratic Administration has not started us on a march to false prosperity and eventual disaster as did the loaning of money abroad during the period from 1920 to 1930. But if the deficit continues too long, the unbalancing of the domestic budget may have an effect as serious as that of our continued foreign-loan and high tariff policy from 1920 to 1930.

It is necessary to take a much broader attitude on the budget than has been taken by the committees of business men who have most to say about it. They have seemed too much interested in petty savings for the purpose of avoiding higher income taxes. Strong and vigorous plans must be made for the eventual balancing of the budget and for the prevention of uncontrolled inflation. But this should not mean the wholesale discharge of faithful and able government servants—the backbone of Federal governmental administration. Neither does it mean that relief should be stopped ruthlessly and at once. It does mean that as prosperity returns a moderately high level of taxation must be retained so that there can be in good times an annual surplus. This surplus can be used for paying off the previous debt or for building a fund to be used in times of depression.

Rules relating to a balanced national budget are much more generally understood than rules relating to an international balance of payments. Even so, millions of persons do not understand the distinct differences between balancing personal budgets and the national budget.

Governments have control of money. This control may properly be used in time of stress; and should be used toward restoring general solvency, and reducing the inequities that result from too-rigid money. This power, not enjoyed by private persons or businesses, gives the Federal Government a certain freedom with regard to budgets, a freedom which cannot exist for individuals, cities, counties, and States. The freedom must be exercised with restraint and with full regard for ultimate results, but it does exist.

A second difference lies in the fact that when individual credit reaches its depression limits there remains a collective credit which only the government can command. If government by using this credit can get our economy off dead-center, the government's own income will be so increased in successive years as to make the temporary lack of budgetary balance good business. But such extensions of credit must be managed to bring us back to a balanced budget. And the breathing spell thus purchased must be utilized with the ultimates in mind.

Another fact not generally revealed in much of the foolishness made public on this question of the national budget, is that the Government does not carry a capital account of the assets it acquires in the process of increasing the national debt. A very large share of the increase in the Government debt under the present administration is represented by assets that can be liquidated, and by tangible permanent assets which ultimately will yield either economic or social income.

The remainder, some would argue, must be balanced immediately. While this is usually sound policy for the individual who has to live from hand to mouth, it is not necessarily sound policy for a government. It may be far from a sound policy for a government whose immediate aim is to start the cycle of recovery and to adjust its budget toward ultimate economic stability. It is not unusual for well-established corporations to plan the liquidation of their long-term debts over a period of 10 years or more. Such a financial policy is even sounder for a government with ultimate objectives of social security in mind.

It should be noted, for the sake of clearer thinking, that the increase in the national debt has been accompanied by a rise in the nation's capacity to pay. Commodity prices, for example, have risen at least a fourth since March 1933; so that in terms of our present dollar there has been a net increase in the national debt of less than 10 per cent. Our national income on an annual basis is now about 10 billion dollars greater than during the first half of 1933, and the annual interest on the increase in the national debt at 3 per cent is only about 210 million dollars, or just about one-fiftieth of the improvement in the national money purchasing power that has been brought about by enlarging the national debt. For a going concern this is not at all discouraging. Yet it should be remembered that this sort of reasoning takes the exceedingly low point of 1933 as a point of departure. I am not anxious to minimize the magnitude of the financial problem that lies ahead of us.

If we can avoid taking rabid views in either direction; if we can sense that government accounts have in them both tangible income-producing assets and permanent social values; if we can see improvement in the national capacity to pay rising out of our building for the future; if we can continue to distinguish between measures of immediate necessity and those of ultimate stability, our budget problem will not stand out as a sore thumb but will be in proper perspective to the much higher volume of physical production and national wealth that we must ultimately attain.

Our great need now is for educated and watchful millions in all the States, for men and women with firmly grounded convictions, who understand the simple arithmetic of the internal budget and the external balance sheet, and who know that any force brought to bear in any way on any single item must be compensated for by some other force.

Democracy desperately needs such an offset to the thousands of special-pleading pressure groups which converge on the Capitol to see how much they can extort for their own short-time interests. The danger of this long-drawn depression is that millions greatly wronged by the inability of the present system to give them work will come to feel that the government owes them a living, and that they, themselves, owe the government nothing. The ideal democracy would, of course, arrange a job for every able-bodied citizen. But in order to build the ideal democracy we need more people who know and are willing to pay the price that must be paid to bring about the harmonious relationship between this nation and other nations externally; and between the parts of this nation internally.

Thousands of civil servants of the Federal Government grasp this attitude instinctively because of the objective position in which they have been placed. But the special pleaders of agriculture, labor, and business continue to cry and contend for special favors. The ideal of understanding allegiance to a common end service has taken as yet but faint hold upon the American imagination.

If our economic machine is to produce adequate and balanced prosperity without regimented adherence to blueprint, we must have men to guide the machine. We must have men who know how to turn out properly for other machines in the dark, who slow up when the roads are rough, and who can make all of the other thousands of compensatory adjustments that must be made by cautious and skillful drivers proceeding over roads new to them.

We of this administration are not committed indefi-

nitely to crop control or to NRA codes. We are committed
to getting the farmer, the laborer, and the industrialist
such share of the national income as will put each in a
balanced relationship with the other. Without such balance the foundation of the state sags. If we can restore
purchasing power for agricultural products by bringing
in more non-agricultural goods from abroad, we may be
able eventually to dispense with crop control. But we
know, for example, that if an American merchant marine
is built up on a scale which reduces our freight payments
to other nations, it will be necessary to increase imports
from abroad just that much more, in order to build up an
effective market for our agricultural surplus.

The hard but necessary first lesson we all must learn is
that we cannot prosper separately. Even individual pressure groups must catch the idea that pressure on behalf
of any individual group makes necessary, sooner or later,
compensating pressure in behalf of other groups. In our
march to a real democracy, governmental powers should
not be loaned too lightly to any group. For the ultimate
security of that loan, there must be clear-cut evidence that
the power will be used to advance a harmonious relationship between forces now contending. The degree to which
this principle can be grasped and applied by business men,
laborers, and farmers reared in a freebooter tradition
remains to be seen. That, as it develops, will set the practical limits of "self-governing industry" and "self-governing agriculture."

In this country nearly all the people can read and write.
Our middle class has a passionate devotion to the national

interest. There is among us a widespread and deep attachment to the democratic principle. Of late years this spirit has been somewhat thwarted and inclined to seek expression in words alone. But the spirit is there and it can be put to work. The intelligence is there and it can be aroused. In this time of continuing crisis I believe there is more than a fighting chance for democracy to prevail.

In particular, the way in which state and county control committees have helped the Agricultural Adjustment Administration carry out acreage control programs leads me to believe that the American people have in them the genius to meet extraordinarily difficult problems in democratic ways. In these programs ninety per cent of the farmers demonstrated that they were honest and conscientious. The farm leaders in the townships and the counties proved beyond all doubt that, generally speaking, they are unselfish and patriotic. Most of the State leaders demonstrated that they were able to catch a national and international vision of what had to be accomplished. They knew that the loss of foreign markets compelled an adjustment. Much of the work was done on a purely voluntary basis.

But while our experience with the educated democracy or county control committees has in general been heartening, we have run into the kind of trouble a modern democracy must always guard against:—petty demagoguery, blind greed. There is no use dodging the fact that the democratic process is full of hazards. Certain politically-minded leaders, thinking only about their own positions, have done some strange things, things which, if typical, would betray any democracy into the hands of the short-time self-seekers, and bring inevitable destruction.

There is, for example, a type of leader who puts himself in a position both of approval and disapproval of the programs we have presented. If the program is adopted, and succeeds, he can point to the approving words. Otherwise, he can point to his other words. One such type of leader has worked with us and ostensibly has taken the attitude of a cooperator; but among those who are critical of what we are doing, he has taken the attitude of a skeptic. His concern has been to keep his position with his organization, come what may.

Still another type of leader has somewhat frankly said that he can best maintain his place with his organization by opposing us. In substance his attitude is, "If I admit that you are doing about as good a job as can be done, there is no place for me in the picture." There is also the farm leader who has had to do some lobbying; his organization has needed revenue other than can be gathered from membership dues; so he has made contacts and formed the habit of playing the lobby game with groups unrelated to agriculture.

In general, the local farm leader is public-spirited. In all of the many organizations of agricultural and near-agricultural character we have many state and national leaders of intelligence, courage, and integrity. But there is a tendency for some of the state and national leaders to become too political. They become addicted to log-rolling and "playing the game"; they become too much concerned about keeping their jobs, and too little concerned about the fundamental and wise determination of policies. I am informed that in the labor and trade association fields the same types of leaders develop.

If our civilization is to continue on the present complex basis, modern democracy must make rules of the game that go beyond tariffs, monetary policy, freight rate structures, taxation and similar policies which have long concerned the central government. The new rules must also get into fields more directly concerning harmonious relationships between prices, margins, profits and distribution of income.

If it seems wise for the central power of a democracy to give a group of corporations the power to fix prices, then it is also wise for the government to have complete access to the books and records of such corporations. In the case of leading corporations dealing with well established processes, it may be necessary to make rules so that consuming power much more nearly and continuously equals productive power. This is a form of the internal budget, in some ways far more important than the Federal Budget about which wealthy income taxpayers are so greatly concerned. A deficit in consuming power of $1,000,000,000 annually may be even more significant than a similar deficit in the Treasury budget.

There was a day when it did not seem essential to be concerned with the facts behind the balance sheets of the great corporations; but when these corporations borrow Federal power and use it in ways that upset the economic balance, the Government has no choice but to take steps to restore and maintain the equilibrium.

For several years an increasing number of businessmen have asked for governmental help in group price-fixing. Such men worked for the passage of the National Industrial Recovery Act and when it became law in June of 1933, they helped write the codes. Many lines of business under the New Deal have thus been able to devote the centralizing power of government to group price-fixing. Farmers and consumers are tremendously interested in knowing just what conditions justify government in permitting business to substitute group price-fixing for competitive price-fixing. Should not the businesses given such privileges submit their books and records to governmental examination? Should not their fixed prices be subject to such governmental control as will promote the most harmonious, continuous, balanced relationship between the different kinds of prices and the maximum employment of labor at just wages?

To do this precisely may be outside the realm of sound government policy. If so, there should be public debate on whether group price-fixing ought to be permitted any group other than the public utilities. This whole problem of group price-fixing may concern us as much from now on as tariff and freight-rate battles concerned us in the past.

Corporations accustomed to influencing government do not like the thought of government influencing them. They are likely to claim that "A Brain Trust is blueprinting a five year plan for industry," or that, "A dictatorship is being set up," or that, "The country is going bolshevik." I agree with the corporations that the government should leave all possible initiative with private citizens and local communities—provided corporations do likewise. But insofar as corporations have transcended localities and have reached out for governmental power, it seems essential for a democracy to develop a mechanism for handling them fairly and in the public interest.

This does not mean "trust baiting" in the old-fashioned sense of the phrase. On occasion, it may mean "trust helping"; but always the primary concern of government must be to direct, restrain, and stimulate the private powers so as to promote balance and continuous stability.

SECOND SECTION

CHANGING THE RULES

INTRODUCTION

THE rules of economic conflict change in response to weird combinations of economics, politics and accidents. Human beings respond far more readily to psychological than to logical arguments. Strange prejudices, which logically have nothing to do with either the present or the future, have been handed down out of the past. People of wealth and influence learn how to prey on these prejudices. Sometimes the demagogues, and newspapers that have learned the same tricks, join hands, under cover, with the wealthy. People listening to the demagogues or reading demagogical statements in the press become excited. They seize upon false issues and waste strength battling for resounding but trifling causes.

In the democracy of tomorrow the people will have to be so intelligently free from prejudice that neither the wealthy, interested in private control of government for personal ends, nor demagogues interested in their jobs, will be able to create deception and illusion. But for many years, it is to be expected that these gentlemen with their many tricks will be trying to change the rules of the game to suit themselves.

Anyone who wants a New Deal must be acquainted with the rules the rogues play by. In the following chapters is some account of old-fashioned tricks they have played in recent months, and a few suggestions for new rules. Social inventors need to become politicians, not only in the fine sense of the word, but in a practical sense. They must study the springs of human nature until, with all the cards on the table, they can beat the old dealers.

The representations made to the government by corporations and business men may be entirely proper, but in dealing with them it is decidedly necessary for the government to have in mind a policy which takes into account long-time considerations from the standpoint of the country as a whole. Modern governments must of necessity consider changing the rules to make for a maximum of balance between producing and consuming forces with the minimum of disturbance to individual liberties. In respect to airplanes, shipping and so on, the governmental influence has also to be exerted with thought of national security in time of war.

Those who try to keep the government from performing this function are short-sighted; they simply do not realize the extent to which pressure groups have for many years tried to appropriate government power for their own ends. The choice is between a hodge-podge, hit or miss application of pressure upon a government which yields here and there, and a more definite recognition of broad national objectives by the government, business men and all the rest of us.

CHAPTER
IV

PRIVATE OWNERSHIP OF GOVERNMENT

WHEN Thomas Jefferson wrote the Declaration of
Independence and evolved his theories of government, 90
per cent of the people were farmers and produced most of
what they consumed in their own community. They sold
little and bought little. Business enterprises were small.
New York was much farther from Virginia in those days
than the United States is from England today.

When the different nations of the world were loose
aggregations of communities, it was easy to reach the conclusion that the central government should be weak, that
the outlying communities should be as independent as
possible, that the power of taxation should be used spar-
ingly, and that tariffs should be levied chiefly for the purpose of either protecting infant industries or raising the
money necessary to pay the interest on debts held by
foreign nations.

Inventions, wars, growth of population, and the development of great corporate enterprises change the situation. Each generation has a different problem. If the rules
are not changed fast enough and in the right direction,
the game eventually breaks up in a riot.

The need for changed rules in the United States has never been so great as since 1920. It was one of the marvels of the world that this country was able to sit in fat complacency with hands folded, doing little to meet a changed world from 1921 to 1932. By 1920 most thoughtful people realized that five disintegrating, yet ultimately beneficent, forces would be acting over a period of at least a generation. These forces are:

1. The end of westward expansion, the gradual reduction in great population increase, and the necessity for meeting unemployment problems more consciously. There is no longer cheap land on which we can thoughtlessly place the unemployed.

2. The rising tide of scientific investigation, inventions, and methods of mass production. This brings sudden and unexpected technological loss of employment, loss of investment and general confusion.

3. The post-war reversal in credit balances between the United States and other nations. Eventually this makes necessary either a reduction in United States exports or an increase in United States imports.

4. The steadily increasing concentration of industrial activity into a few great corporations. This has almost destroyed the effectiveness of the old-fashioned free-play of the market place.

5. The decentralizing effect of a loaded freight-rate structure, shattering as a result of developing highway transportation.

These great forces have come to the front in the United States since the World War. On each of them many books might be written. The pioneer path of the American people came to an abrupt end in 1914. To keen students necessity for changing rules in conformity to a new age was apparent in 1920. The psychology of the American people is still not greatly different from what it was in 1914, and this is not surprising. All peoples change slowly in their traditional attitudes, and no nation has ever been called on to make such extraordinary changes in such a short time as the United States. It is not at all surprising that wealthy and powerful groups in control in 1914 and still in control in 1932 should do their best to make the American people think their rules of the good old days should be continued today.

The big business men of the United States who live in the great trading and financial centers like New York and Chicago are continually talking about the dangers of governmental interference with business. The smaller businessmen of the United States in their Chambers of Commerce and the noonday luncheon clubs continually say there should be "less government in business and more business in government."

As a matter of fact, certain businesses have always been up to their necks in government. This is especially true of the central core of the banking business and those businesses which, from a world competitive point of view, are so inefficient that they would die without tariff protection.

The old-timers hold up their hands in horror at the thought of government regulation or ownership of business. It is a truism that any startling new development is usually the result of the extraordinary insight and hard work of some one man, and of those who have been set on fire by his example. It is to be hoped that the government will never do anything to discourage the ardor or the insight of those individuals who, we trust in the future as in the past, will carry the banner of inventive, American business genius. We do not want such individuals shackled by governmental red tape.

But it should be mentioned in passing that governmental red tape and bureaucracy are no worse than corporate red tape and bureaucracy after the original founding and inspiring individuals have passed out of the picture. Governmental political graft and intrigue are no worse than corporate political graft and intrigue. The order of ability of governmental employees averages at least as high as that of the corporate employees. The attack on governmental expenditures and governmental employees as conducted by big business groups interested in lowering income taxes in the early thirties was in many particulars bitterly unfair.

The United States has suffered fully as much in the past from the private regulation of government as it has from the government regulation of business. Private control of government in the United States began with Alexander Hamilton, and has continued. Hamilton sincerely believed that the wealth and power of the United States should be strongly centralized in the hands of an aristocratic few. As the first Secretary of the Treasury, he bent every effort to tie the strong, influential, wealthy people in each community to the new government. By using the power of the government, he made it possible to redeem certain debts and bonds at par. Thus he made most of the wealthy individuals in the various communities feel greatly indebted to the central government.

Hamilton did not profit in a personal, financial sense from his policy but he undoubtedly used the power of government for certain special classes. He favored tariffs on manufactured goods which would serve to tie the great manufacturing interest to the central government.

Most people believe that the Hamiltonian theory of developing government policy so as to tie the strong, influential, propertied individuals to it, was an essential part of launching the new nation under the Constitution. The Hamiltonian theory was adopted by the Republican party after the Civil War, and expanded. More and more the big banking houses assumed as a matter of course that they and the government were essentially one in the matter of monetary and financial policies. Their men were placed in the Treasury as a matter of course. It was important that government bonds be issued at the right time, in the right quantity, and bearing the right rate of interest in order that the financial structure of the country might not be disturbed and in order that banking and national prosperity should be properly conserved. All of this is natural enough, and perhaps to some extent unavoidable.

But if the full truth were ever known about the way in which government influence has been used by great corporations, public indignation would know no bounds. I call to mind a devout wealthy Pennsylvanian who was ruined some years ago because a great corporation used its influence in a totally unjustifiable way with the office of the Comptroller of the Currency. Men experienced in government at Washington will understand by this time the extent to which certain, but not all, American corporations dealing with munitions,* shipping, airplane and airmail subsidies, and oil rights, have tried and often succeeded in using their power over government for flagrantly anti-social ends. Nearly every President who has had anything to do with tariff revision has been impressed by the way great businesses rally 'round in the hope of securing governmental favors through the tariff in order to help them promote monopolies. Such legalized thievery is probably working more harm to the people of the United States than all other forms of robbery put together.

Those smaller men who sit at home attending quietly to their own business and who never come near Washington, either personally or through the secretary of their association, do not realize the extent to which we have always had private control of government. Larger businessmen and the paid secretaries are continually trying to change the rules of the economic scramble. Hundreds of them are on the job every day whether Congress is in session or not. They are just as active when the Democrats are in power as when the Republicans are in. Perhaps the majority of them are not seeking unfair advantages. Many

* The following quotation from a letter written by a munitions lobbyist indicates how one man in 1929 felt that one particular private industry had come into friendly control of certain functions of five governmental departments:

"With good will and a friendly attitude existing in the Army and Navy, in Commerce and shipping board, and the Treasury department, and a good will does exist, which is true as is the statement of friendly relations, we may well feel that a brighter future has opened up for this company, with less sales resistance, and pleasant hours free from past worries and cares. . . . The writer wishes every one in the organization without exception to feel and to know that all have played a part in loyalty, kind considerations and co-operation, and that they are entitled to share the pleasure and delight in the final victory, and in my humbleness desire to express my sincere thanks to all." STERLING J. JOYNER.

are merely trying to protect themselves so that some one else does not get there first.

Some day some one will write the story of the lawyer lobbyists in Washington. Many of them held high positions in the government five, ten or fifteen years ago. They learned the ropes, and when they went out of office they found that they could use their knowledge of governmental procedure to good advantage as the servants of businessmen who want to get something out of the government. They are among the most pleasant people in Washington. Many of them have very high personal standards and have never urged on the government action which goes beyond fairness; others belong in about the same category as Al Capone and Dillinger. These last have no sense of fairness or understanding and are out to represent their clients by strong-arm political methods.

When the codes were fixed up under NRA, businessmen came to Washington by the thousands, most of them hoping to get codes fixed so that their competitors would not have an unfair advantage. Many of them hoped that they might be able to get hold of governmental power in order to put their competitors out of business. They wanted the government to help them fix prices and control production.

Of course, businessmen are not alone in this wish. In recent years both farm organizations and labor organizations have also been doing their best to get hold of governmental power for their own purposes. As these interests begin to fight each other more and more, it will become apparent that the old game is played out. A new one with new rules must be arranged.

With the situation as it is today, it is foolish to talk about either government regulation of business or private regulation of government as a major issue. Every day for a number of years, government must work more and more with business, labor, agriculture and consumers. When business came to the government in the old days for tariff legislation, the loan of banking control, railroad land grants, and corporation laws, it admitted that it was going to be a partner with the government in a way altogether beyond that envisioned by Thomas Jefferson and Adam Smith.

We may not like it, but the hard facts are that for years government has been in business, and business in government, to a point where it is impossible to untangle the mess.

The policy of partnership between government and business was started long before the Great War, as a result very largely of the Republican attitude on tariff, money and railroads. The important thing now is to find some sensible way of working together.

If we are not to go in for Communism or Fascism, it is essential that government learn to look on itself as a partner with business, labor, agriculture and consumers. For the sake of campaign funds, governments have all too often handed out jobs and passed out favors. The Republican party has had somewhat the best of this kind of game because its historic tariff attitude made possible a perennial shakedown of the wealthy, inefficient, monopolistic industries.

It is time for business to stop speaking scornfully of government in business and then go running to it in private to see what it can get out of the government. Will Rogers noted this phenomenon in one of his newspaper contributions when he said:

San Francisco, Cal., May 2, 1934—
—See where the United States Chamber of Commerce is gathered in Washington again. It's the caviar of big business. Last time they met I happened to be in Washington and was the guest of Jesse Jones (head of the Reconstruction Finance) at their dinner. Now the whole constitution, by-laws and secret ritual of that orchid club is to "keep the government out of business."

Well that's all right, for every organization must have a purpose, but here was the joke, they introduced all the big financiers, the head of this, that and the other. As each stood up, Jesse would write on the back of the menu card just what he had loaned him from the RFC (I got that menu card yet). Yes, they said "keep the government out of business."

Government and business must learn to live together in a sensible way. In working out the terms of this partnership, it is important that not only the big businessmen who have always made their voices heard in Washington be consulted, but that the small businessmen, laboring men, farmers and consumers, also be in on the deal.

The object is a continually moving, but balanced state. European purchasing power for our surplus is shattered. We still have great adjustments to make before we can safely face that fact. Men of all classes realize the need of readjustment. Many leaders in government recognize it. But unfortunately we still have in government and among businessmen many who are most interested in the short time turns of the profit wheel.

Some of these men know how to trim their sales so suddenly that they can profit just as well during a depression as during a boom. They are ghouls fattening on human disaster. Many of them keep their wealth fluid so that they can shift it rapidly from country to country. In time of inflation, they pass their wealth rapidly into commodities. They may have no lobbyists in Washington, but they keep in close touch with governmental policies so that they can shift their wealth to the best advantage. They talk about lower income taxes, less government in business, and less governmental bureaucracy, but they have no fundamental interest in the long-time prosperity of the country.

CHAPTER

V

PERSONAL DEVILS

CHANGING the rules is usually accompanied by the exorcising of personal devils. Sometimes people become so fascinated by their devils that they forget they set out to change the rules.

Indeed, one of the greatest handicaps to a smoothly functioning, intelligent democracy is the almost universal belief in personal devils. Most Americans until recently have believed in the innate wickedness of nearly all countries other than our own. The French, British, Japanese, Germans, Russians, and Italians have all been pictured as devils at one time or another. European nations owed us money and didn't pay. The American people without thinking the matter through cried instinctively, "Make the devils pay!"

Farmers have long fought many personal devils. Forty years ago their favorite one was the railroads. But the railroad devil which seemed so tremendous and threatening to the farmers until 1922 finally shrunk to rather small size during the depression, in spite of the fact that since 1930 railroad rates have been proportionately more burdensome than at any time during the past thirty-five years.

At one time the railroads seemed to be the focal point of monopoly control. Both the agricultural and financial interests recognized this and there were continuous battles from 1890 to 1920 between groups representing the railroad and anti-railroad point of view. The people in the central parts of the country had very strong feelings about the way railroad rates were modified to build certain great centers of population. When, in the 20's, trucks, autos and hard roads broke definitely any possibility of absolute transportation monopoly by the railroads, the farm folks continued for some time to kick the old devil even though he was sick and half dead.

More continuously interesting to farm people is the Wall Street devil with its presumed control of the money power. It has been assumed that the speculators of Wall Street have spent much of their time behind closed doors conniving how they could skin the farmer and small business man. The Chicago Board of Trade devil has customarily been supposed to be a brother of the Wall Street devil and working in cahoots with him.

The Wall Street devil got sick in 1930 and in 1933 and 1934 the Federal Government tied him down, cut off his horns and branded him so he could no longer exercise his money power in the old-fashioned way. The Board of Trade devil had a halter put on him in 1922 in the Grain Futures Act but when an effort was made to cut his horns off by passing a more definite law in 1934, a legislator who apparently did not wish to see record kept of large speculative transactions in cotton, enabled this particular devil to jump over the fence and escape for the time being.

One of the most popular of the personal devils from the

standpoint of people who run for office is the middleman devil. What happens to food from the time it leaves the farmers' hands until it reaches the consumers' plates? The railroads, commission men, processors, wholesalers, and retailers now take nearly twice as much for their services as they did before the war. The farmer may get bankruptcy prices or be unable to sell at all, at a time when consumers feel that prices are so high that they are unable to buy. Therefore, it is said that the middleman is a devil, that he profiteers, that he destroys food to keep up prices, and that he enters into collusive arrangements. Some of these things are occasionally true, and as both farmers and consumers like to hear the story, there are always plenty of politicians and newspapers ready to denounce the middleman devil.

During the past ten or fifteen years, the red devil has been the outstanding favorite among businessmen. The red devil came from Russia and carries the brand of Marx and Lenin. If anyone in government service says anything which businessmen do not like, they hold up the red devil to scare the people. Some businessmen and certain Congressmen really believe in the red devil, but most of them use him because they think this is an easy way to scare people so they will not give real thought to social and economic problems. For my part, I abhor the bitterness and violence which characterize the Communistic approach to economic problems, and for that reason I feel that it is bad theology to use the red devil indiscriminately to serve the ends of business.

The whole devil business, although providing a focal point for enthusiasm, often interferes with hard thinking and clean-cut action. Devil-shouting may be useful in gaining votes or increasing the circulation of a newspaper or tightening the hold of an unscrupulous leader on his organization, but it alone is of very little help in cleaning up the mess. The devil-shouters are dynamic speech-makers and sometimes are excellent writers of magazine articles. They sometimes arouse the public about abuses, but beyond that their usefulness ends.

It is necessary eventually to get beyond name-calling which rouses human passions but prevents thinking and delays action. Modern democracy cannot be effective until our people are willing to support leaders capable of going beyond calling each other names.

When we treat the money power as a devil and try to put him in jail and torture him, we all too often hurt ourselves tenfold. The evils in our faulty money system have caused us great harm. But in order to get rid of the evils we must go on to a definite careful measured under-standing of our problem. It will not do us a particle of good to assume that the bankers and speculators are trying to suck our life blood and that therefore we should destroy them and their works. In this direction lies either futility or a revolution which will destroy many, but which will eventually build up another system with probably even greater abuses. Devil-baiting does not lead to an under-standing of economic forces any more than the ducking of witches improved the morals of the early colonists. We did not get far with the treatment of malaria as long as we believed in the theory that disease was caused by evil spirits and the way to get rid of disease was to scare out the spirits. Real progress came only when we used quinine and got rid of mosquitoes. In approaching economic problems most of us are still in the old witch-doctor days.

The real iniquity of most of the devils lies in the fact that they distort judgment and misuse power. The margin charged and the wealth gained by the devils is not necessarily serious but the way power is used by the devils in the direction and control of economic forces may bring disaster.

Those of us who have grown up fighting the evils which our pet devils represent should for the most part continue the fight, perhaps relaxing our efforts against a few antiquated ones and favoring some of the newer ones with more vigorous punches. Perhaps if we had attacked them scientifically, and more impersonally, we might have plucked more horns and pronged tails and left fewer for the present generation to worry about. The present generation, on whose shoulders falls the task of building beyond the new frontiers should select their own causes to fight for as they go through life. Having a cause to fight for, even if it takes the form of a personal devil, lends zest to life and assures a greater measure of accomplishment. But the oncoming generation must avoid inheriting those of their father's personal devils whose powers have been spent. There are still vigorous ones and ever new ones whose aims are selfish and whose eyes see not. They should be fought not merely with passion, but with understanding of the forces that begot them.

CHAPTER
VI

HOT SPOTS, PRESSURE GROUPS
AND NEWS DRIVES

THOSE who in the past have sought a change in the rules have not limited themselves to wishing for it, or to passing fervent resolutions. They have worked for the change, sometimes openly and fairly, sometimes secretly and deviously. It seems to me essential that we understand how these things are done. We should reject the bad and make use of the good technique, but we ought to be aware of the existence of both.

The rise and fall of political pressure is something like the weather. When economic conditions are bad, the political situation will be hot and sultry. Then the thunder clouds will roll up, flashing with lightning. The clouds may pass away without result, or there may be an abundant rain of government credit or cash.

Congressmen, Senators and the people who are in administrative positions are fully familiar with the technique we may call hot spots, pressure groups, and news drives. But 99 per cent of the people who depend for their understanding on what they read would be amazed if they

could see the method at first-hand. The injudicious use
of these methods may eventually cause the United States
to follow Rome into history. Insofar as these methods are
used to awaken a sleepy Government to its fundamental
responsibilities, there can be no sound criticism. Energetic, yet selfish people thinking solely about short-time
or regional objectives put on drive after drive.

One of the most interesting political thunderstorms I
ever watched was that which precipitated the five Northwestern Governors upon Washington in November, 1933.
Farm prices, after the skyrocket speculative advance in
midsummer of 1933, had sagged during the fall so that
there was tremendous dissatisfaction among the farmers
who a few months earlier thought that their troubles had
suddenly and miraculously come to an end. The NRA
had increased the cost of the things the farmers purchase
at the very time that their own products had gone down
greatly in price. There was great indignation in many
communities, and this was capitalized by the leaders of
the Farm Holiday movement who preached far and wide
that it was the duty of the government to fix farm product
prices at a high level. They were so energetic that certain
of the Governors of the Northwest thought there ought to
be a farm meeting. The meeting was held, resolutions
were adopted, and the five Northwestern Governors agreed
to go down to Washington to see what could be done to
bring about a code for agriculture and to fix prices.

When the Governors arrived in Washington, it was
apparent that at least four of them were sincerely anxious
to do something for agriculture. They really thought that
an agricultural code should be adopted which would en-

able farmers to get cost of production in the same way
that the lumber manufacturers were getting cost of production out of their code. When this matter was looked
into, it was discovered that in the National Recovery Act
there is a provision known as the Huey Long amendment
which makes it impossible to interfere with the free marketing rights of the individual farmer or laboring man.

The Governors then suggested that we move at once
under the Agricultural Adjustment Act to fix prices. They
wanted us to license the packers to pay at least $8 per hun-
dred for hogs and everything else in proportion. They
wanted us to double and treble farm product prices at
once by the simple method of licensing all processors and
dealers so that they could not purchase farm products except at a very much higher price.

It was suggested that this might be illegal or unconstitu-
tional, but one Governor spoke up with the brusque statement, "Hell, what's the Constitution between friends?"

It was then suggested that only two-thirds as many
pounds of hog products could be passed into consumption
at $8 a hundred as at the price then prevailing, and it
would, therefore, be necessary in order to carry out the
program of licensing the dealers and processors to determine a quota for every individual farmer. We asked the
Governors if they were ready to stand for compulsory control of the quotas of each individual farmer. Then they
began to doubt whether they wanted to regiment the entire range of agriculture all at once.

The Governors had been put on the spot by certain
farm spellbinders who had an opening because of the increase in prices under the NRA at a time when farm prod-

uct prices were dropping. Instead of trying to think the problem through, for the country_as a whole, they had allowed themselves to be persuaded of the practicability of price-fixing, and they came down to Washington to put the Administration on the spot instead of themselves.

Politically they were in much stronger position than we were. Their program sounded reasonable to the farmers who had been suffering most unfairly for many years. They came from five farm States; we had to take a national view. We knew we would get into a terrible mess if we attempted to go along with the Governors. If they had had something which was really practical and well-thought-out, the answer might have been much different.

One of the most beneficial pressure drives was led by Southern Senators and Congressmen in an effort to get a higher price for cotton in the late summer of 1933. Cotton prices, like all others, had gone down suddenly in price during the late summer and early fall of 1933, and the Southerners were determined that something should be done about it. A group of about thirty of them came to my office to make speeches. They wanted the price of cotton fixed at once by the government at 15¢ a pound. They wanted the government to buy cotton at 15¢ a pound or to loan money on cotton at 15¢ a pound.

We didn't want to loan 15¢ a pound on cotton because we believed that this would encourage foreign cotton-growing countries to expand their acreage altogether too much. Under the Adjustment program, we were selling cotton abroad on a world basis without any processing tax included, which meant that the American cotton farmer was getting for his crop the world's price plus about 4¢ a pound in addition on the domestically consumed portion of the crop. Inasmuch as 60 per cent of the cotton is normally exported, we didn't like to see the government take any action which would limit exports. We still had a carryover of nearly three times the normal and we felt that this had to be whittled down by exporting as much cotton as possible out of the country.

At the same time, we recognized that there had been altogether too great a drop in farm produce prices during the late summer and fall of 1933 and that insofar as possible, we should do something about it. We believed, furthermore, that the prices would be higher by the summer of 1934. We therefore suggested that we would take up with the President the desirability of loaning without recourse 10¢ a pound on cotton on the farm, thus putting an effective peg under the cotton market.

As a result of the stimulus furnished to the Administration by the Southern Senators, Congressmen, and farm leaders, the Commodity Credit Corporation was formed and loans without recourse were made not only on cotton but also on corn to producers who agreed to participate in the 1934 adjustment programs.

This radical and seemingly unbusinesslike procedure was, in my opinion, abundantly justified in the fall of 1933 by the special conditions prevailing at that time. This particular pressure drive, which resulted in the loaning of $240,000,000 to corn and cotton farmers, has probably saved them over the past year more than $80,000,000 which otherwise would have gone to speculators and others less entitled to the money. Undoubtedly prices during the winter of 1933-1934 would have gone much lower if it had not been for these loans. We kept corn and cotton in farmers' hands so that they, not speculators, could get the benefit of any increase. With the monetary policy as it was in the fall of 1933 and with our production control program just getting started, it seemed to us that we were safe in endeavoring to put a bottom under the market of these fundamental crops. The fact that we did not make the loans except to those farmers who agreed to engage in a production control program made the loans economically sound.

One of the most extraordinary pressure groups which ever operated in Washington was formed in the fall of 1932 under the name of the Committee for the Nation. This group, composed largely of business men interested in the export trade, genuinely felt that the prosperity of the United States would be greatly enhanced if the price of gold could be raised in terms of dollars. In vigorously worded circulars they issued information and arguments favorable to this point of view and enrolled some of the most prominent business men of the Nation as members.

The Committee's program was in line with the trend of the times. For a while it seemed to the general public that the Committee had made progress. But after the price of gold had been raised to $35 an ounce, it began to appear that the Committee perhaps was more interested in the Wall Street point of view than the fundamental program of the Administration. It was this feeling on the part of some of the leaders in the Committee for the Nation which precipitated one of the most comical news drives the Nation has ever seen—the Wirt incident.

After occupying the limelight and being apparently successful in attaining its objectives during a considerable part of 1933, the Committee for the Nation seemed to feel its importance slipping away. The failure of various blessings which the committee had promised would happen, if only gold prices were raised, left it in need of new devices not too patently remodeled. Some of the members seemed to be anxious for speculative prices to go higher and felt that the prosperity of the United States was dependent on the lack of regulation of the Stock Exchange. James Rand, the president of the Committee for the Nation, apparently felt that the true function of Government was to raise the price of gold and not to concern itself with other matters. He and his friend, Dr. Wirt, raised the cry of the Red Menace. Apparently they believed sincerely that continually higher prices obtained by monetary means would destroy the Red Menace and make the United States safe for speculative business men and real estate operators in the true spirit of 1929.

They were interested in changing the rules of the game with respect to money but not with respect to anything else. For a time they received astounding support, especially from certain reactionary newspapers, in their publicity drive to create a public psychology against the changing of any rules of the game except the money rules. But this particular drive got completely out of hand and entertained the Nation with one of the most spectacular farces of recent years.

The tremendous danger of special pressure groups is that they will persuade sympathetic governmental officials to do things which are fundamentally unsound. Almost invariably a pressure group asks for far more than it is entitled to. It is thinking about the political implications of the headlines in the newspapers the following morning.

An informing glimpse of a strong pressure group at work undeterred by the opposition of the most popular President of recent times may be had from the following news account in *The New York Times* of March 29, 1934. The House had overridden the President's veto of the Independent Offices Bill, which bill carried a rider greatly increasing pensions and allowances to veterans. The Senate was now, also about to override the veto, with a vote of 63 to 27. It was quite a spectacle:

"—During the course of the debate," (*The Times* reports), Senators could be seen leaving the chamber to confer in the anterooms with lobbyists on both sides of the question, while a number of times Rice W. Means of Colorado, Commander of the United Spanish War Veterans, availed himself of his privilege as a former member of the Senate to confer with his former colleagues. . . . With a former Senator using the privileges of the floor, the veteran's lobby worked at high speed today all during the debate.——"

There is a demagogic, chauvinistic segment of the American press which distorts facts by editorializing its news columns. Fortunately its influence is small, in spite of its noise and bombast. But occasionally the methods it follows can be somewhat embarrassing, especially when it pushes news drives that arouse the special prejudices of a particular group or section. An illustration of this was the American shipping drive started in the late summer of

1934 by a chain of papers which quoted from a letter of mine to a Virginia Congressman from a ship building district. In his letter to me, he had listed some of the arguments he thought might legitimately be taken into account on behalf of special government help to shipping. In reply I suggested that in addition to the considerations mentioned by him, account should be taken also of the fact that a further reduction in payment to foreign nations for shipping services would make it necessary for us correspondingly to increase imports from abroad or decrease exports. This letter of mine was not released to the public from my office, but a month after it was written some reporter apparently was given excerpts by the Congressman. The news drive which then was started completely ignored the fact that I recognized in my letter the need for a balanced approach. By partial quotation from my letter, the shipping interest was worked into a great lather. Several usually well-balanced men made statements based on the false premise which, like a man of straw, had been set up to be pummeled. Many people must have thought that the heat of August dog days had driven either the newspaper chain or the Secretary of Agriculture crazy. Millions of good people in humble circumstances, unfamiliar with the methods employed by the demagogic section of the press to distort facts, are thus equipped with prejudices which increase hatred and greed, and make increasingly difficult, for the people as a whole, a calm, balanced approach to public questions.

Often a pressure group after a few meetings out in the country, comes down to Washington with Congressional and Senatorial representation, works out a news release, calls in some reporters, (whose job, of course, is to report whatever of interest that happens), goes over to the government department involved, and releases the news story immediately after having made the call. They figure that in this way the department involved will be put most effectively on the spot, and that it will then have to come through with effective action or else stand before the country convicted of being unsympathetic.

The old Farm Board was put terribly on the spot with special drives of this sort. The economists with the Farm Board knew better than to get mixed up with the purchase of millions of bushels of wheat by the government at over a dollar a bushel as long as they had no mechanism for controlling the size of the subsequent crops. They tried to avoid it, but the political pressure of falling prices was too great. Millions of dollars of government money were thus wasted in a completely fruitless endeavor even though prices were held up for the time being.

The Agricultural Adjustment Administration will undoubtedly find itself up against many similar drives during the next year. Inasmuch as the lending of 10¢ a pound on cotton and 45¢ a bushel on corn in the fall of 1933 turned out to be so satisfactory, certain groups in the future will probably put on drives to get us to lend unduly large amounts. Such drives may be very popular politically, and those leading them may gain votes for themselves, although they would stand convicted in the eyes of those who understand the economics of the situation as weak, ignorant or unscrupulous.

Frankly, I am skeptical about loans at a high figure in short crop years.

As a rule, isn't it better to loan chiefly in years of large crops, and if it turns out that the Government has to take over the product on which it has loaned, should not the government-owned product be used instead of cash to pay benefit payments the following year to those farmers who cooperate in a reduction control program? In this way the Government should be able to operate as a stabilizing force both from the standpoint of price from year to year and from the standpoint of a more uniform supply.

This philosophy, which seems to me to have in it much of fundamental importance, was derived, in part, as the result of the thinking caused by one of the pressure groups.

The sugar lobby in Washington has always been one of the most skillful of the pressure groups. When I declined to recommend to the President the signing of the sugar agreement in October of 1933, there was launched a powerful attack from many different angles. The agreement they had proposed was especially designed to increase the profits of American sugar refiners and had practically nothing to do, in my opinion, with the growers of sugar beets.

The merits of the case did not enter into their drive, however. Both Republican and Democratic politicians were turned loose on the Department of Agriculture. Representatives of growers whose minds had been seduced with the most astounding stories made astonishing statements. A high-priced publicity man was engaged to place advertising in the places where it would do the most good. Strong western newspapers entered into a concerted drive.

I had been forewarned of the campaign funds gathered

for this purpose, so this particular political thundercloud had much the same effect on me as the thunder and lightning that you see on the stage. We went steadily ahead on what we believed to be a fundamentally sound sugar program which would do justice to the American producers of sugar but which would not permit them to expand their business further at the expense of 125 million people, and which would not confer on the American refiners a special privilege, for which the Agricultural Adjustment Act was not designed.

There are certain people living in Washington who have learned to make a specialty out of what might almost be called political blackmail. Some of them are representatives of well-organized associations. They have been in Washington so long that they call Congressmen by their first names. They are acquainted with all the special cliques and know how to start a flock of telegrams rolling upon Washington at the right time. They can get close friends on the floor of the House or Senate to interpose an objection in committee meetings, or on the floor, at a time when it will cause embarrassment.

These lobbyists and legislative representatives are usually very pleasant and well liked, but all too often they have their minds fixed on a special regional, short-time objective, and are often more ruthless and unfair than the people who employ them. They feel that they must make a special showing of having done things in the interest of a particular small group in order that that small group will feel warranted in continuing their salaries for the following year.

These people in one way and another manufacture an

astonishing part of the public sentiment which is supposed to rise from the grass roots. By creating situations they also produce much of the news which comes out of Washington. Most of the newspapers try to keep clear of entangling affiliations with a narrow group, but some of them, even in quite sizable cities, deliberately serve a very special group and distort the news accordingly.

The alarming thing in Washington is not that there are so many special pressure groups but that there are so few people who are concerned solely with looking at the picture from the broad, national angle. Most Congressmen and Senators, it seems, are of necessity special pleaders for a particular region. It is, therefore, up to the executive branch of the Government to consider the national interest. This is difficult at times because many officials in the executive branch owe their positions to representations made by particular Congressmen or Senators at the behest of special groups. It is my observation, however, that the executive branch of the Government has astonishingly high standards and unusual capacity to detect the difference between the legitimate and the illegitimate political drives. And it must not be forgotten that while members of Congress often become members of pressure groups they also are continually under pressure, much of which they courageously resist.

CHAPTER
VII

THE TARIFF

PIONEERS always owe money to older settled sections. As soon as they have built their houses, barns, factories and roads, they must begin to ship out more stuff than they import. An excess of exports over imports is used, in effect, to pay the interest on the debts. In the settlement of America much of the pioneer debt was held abroad.

Eager to assert their independent positions in the world, young pioneer nations usually encourage their industries by means of tariffs. High tariffs in a debtor nation force the people there to buy less goods from abroad. At the same time their own sheltered expansion of infant industries continues until they can supply the domestic market.

Before the World War the United States was a debtor nation and a believer in high tariffs. American tariffs have always been extraordinarily high. In Democratic administrations they have not been quite as high as in Republican administrations, but from the standpoint of practical action, it is true that previous to the great war both Democrats and Republicans were high-tariff.

As the United States began to mature, however, and as

infant industries grew into giants, the Democrats and Progressive Republicans became increasingly doubtful about those tariffs which fostered vast monopolies. Both Democrats and Progressive Republicans still believed in tariffs, but they began to question whether the tariff rules should be made in such a way as to enrich unfairly one particular group of people at the expense of another.

We cannot safely put off decision on the tariff question forever. What are the proper tariff rules from the standpoint of a pioneer debtor nation, a mature creditor nation and the entire world?

After the War of 1812 it was quite natural for manufacturers of the United States who had obtained a good start during the war to ask for protection against the dumping of British goods. After the Civil War, when we borrowed enormous quantities of money from Europe to build our railroads, it was decidedly natural to arrange our tariffs so that we bought very little from Europe and sold her a great deal. Again, in the fight on the Payne-Aldrich Tariff Bill in 1909 it was natural for the progressive leaders of the country to cry out that the government had gone too far in giving high tariffs to raise the prices and enhance the profits of large industrial concerns.

When the World War ended, all informed and sensible people knew that it would be only a question of time until the United States as a mature creditor nation would have to change her tariff rules. A mature nation is one whose population is nearing the stationary mark and whose factory facilities are large enough to exploit the natural resources, both physical and human, with a fair degree of effectiveness. A creditor nation is one which must currently import more goods and services than it exports, unless its current loans are greater than the interest due it. The latter, of course, cannot continue indefinitely without default on old loans.

After a time, a mature creditor nation is absolutely forced to lower its tariffs, or to cancel (or face default on) the debts owed from abroad, or to cut down on its exports, or perhaps all three. Certain types of expenditures on services furnished by foreign countries may help toward balance, but these alone are not likely to be sufficient. Loaning money abroad, whether it be done directly or indirectly by devaluing the dollar, postpones for only a few years the fundamental show-down.

Politicians should have realized in 1919 that our tariff rules would have to be changed to encourage importations. Some did, but unfortunately most politicians have to give more thought to human nature as it is today than to the inevitable trend of economic forces tomorrow. That is why we have the insane spectacle of tariffs raised in 1922 and again in 1930, in defiance of the inevitable fundamental trend of the American post-war position.

You have heard the customary argument for the tariff: that our high standard of living results from it. In the old days it was said that we must have a tariff sufficiently great to measure the difference in the cost of production at home and abroad. It was said that if the tariff were high enough to protect our high-cost producers from the low-cost producers abroad, our general standard of living would be higher. The Tariff Commission has solemnly made many investigations as to cost of production of different commodities here and abroad. The commissioners knew, all the while, that their findings would eventually be governed for the most part by personal and regional consideration of private benefit. The cost of production theory in tariff making was merely a convenient political dodge.

An extreme illustration of the foolishness of the theory would be furnished if certain individuals growing bananas in greenhouses in the United States were to ask the Tariff Commission (assuming that there was a tariff on bananas) for an increase sufficient to measure the difference in cost of producing bananas in the United States and in Central America.

Or suppose that as a result of Department of Agriculture experiments indicating that we can produce rubber in the United States from guayule for 30¢ a pound, Congress places a tariff on rubber of 15¢ a pound. Rubber producers then undertake to prove that the domestic costs are really 40¢ a pound, that the foreign costs are only 15¢ a pound, and that the tariff should be raised. As another argument for the American public, they would doubtless point out that they were paying their labor $30 a week, whereas the coolie labor of the East Indies is getting only a small fraction of that amount. They would raise the cry, "We must protect the American standards of living from the Orientals who live on three cents worth of rice a day, dress only in a loin cloth and sleep under thatched roofs." This illustration is not impossibly fantastic. We have in the United States today highly protected industries which are relatively as inefficient as the rubber industry would be. And these industrialists lament concerning the threat to the American standard of living, and weep continuously. They shudder to think what would happen if the tariff on their own inefficiently produced product were lowered.

The fact is that our high standard of living in the United States is not a result of the tariff. The fundamental cause is simply that we have a small, efficient population relative to huge natural resources. Our efficient industries, the ones that do not need tariffs, have always led the way toward wage increases. The inefficient tariff-protected industries have resisted wage increase most bitterly.

No part of the world is so abundantly equipped with the fundamental necessities for civilization. Comparable parts of Europe are so densely populated that it is impossible for an hour of man-labor there to turn out as large quantities of the good things of life as we do here. In a broad, general way the physical standard of living in the United States can exceed the standard in foreign countries only to the extent that our labor turns out more goods than the labor of other men does elsewhere. In parts of Europe and the Orient, labor may receive only one-fourth or even one-tenth of United States wages, but the output of labor per hour in these regions is likely to be so low as largely to counteract the effect of the low wages.

Of course, there are certain specialty manufacturers, not dependent for their efficiency primarily on the abundance of raw material and methods of mass production, which can employ this cheap labor and put out knick-knacks more cheaply than similar specialty manufacturers in the United States today.

When we were a debtor nation, it may have been wise to shut out imports. To do so made more certain an excess of exports with which to reduce our indebtedness and increase our prosperity. But today we are among creditor nations a fettered giant; and the logic of our present position will demand more and more that we admit increasing quantities of goods. Preferably these should be products in which the American advantages of great natural resources and advanced methods of mass production do not count.

There are many goods not of fundamental importance in time of war, goods involving large amounts of hand labor, or goods of æsthetic value which might well be imported in larger quantities from abroad. America as a whole would be greatly benefited by such increased imports.

At the same time it must be admitted that there are certain regions and certain industries which might be harmed. The change, therefore, should be made gradually at that time when the rising tide of prosperity in the United States makes it possible for us to absorb the increased quantities of imports. In 1928 and 1929 at the high tide of our prosperity, we imported more than three times as much goods in dollars as we did at the low time of the depression in 1932.

Larger imports would give our people in the United States more physical goods to consume. Our laboring people would be more completely employed in our efficient industries. Their wages would buy more of the good things of life. Countries with large populations and small natural resources will always have relatively low wages. Such countries, with cheap labor, can produce knick-knacks, the handmade, the artisan or folk type of product to the best advantage.

It would seem the part of wisdom for us to exchange the goods we can produce more efficiently than anyone else in the world for goods that foreign peoples can produce more cheaply than we. There is no reason why we, with our high-priced labor, should go extensively into the production of oriental rugs, cloisonne vases, fancy embroidery, or other products involving a vast amount of very cheap hand labor, and inherited capacities from a far past. As long as our housewives get satisfaction out of this sort of thing, why isn't it good for all concerned to give foreigners in exchange for such products our surplus of the things which we can produce so easily and well?

In the 19th century Great Britain became a mature creditor nation. Sensibly she chose the policy of exporting manufactured goods and importing raw materials. A mature creditor nation in this 20th century, the United States has a much more difficult problem. We have surpluses of many kinds of raw materials and of many kinds of manufactured goods.

We are such a wealthy nation, on paper and in prospect; and we have passed so suddenly from the role of debtor to leading creditor in the world community, that we haven't been able since 1918 to make up our mind just what we would like to accept from abroad. Of course, we have been willing to accept our customary quantities of sugar, coffee, tea, and silk. But the value of these products combined with what our tourists ordinarily spend abroad has not been enough to enable the foreign nations to buy the goods which we have now available for export, and in addition pay the interest which the foreign nations owe us because of their debt. We must find other kinds of goods which we are willing to accept.

If we can find goods which American consumers prefer in their homes, national prejudices notwithstanding, such goods will cost us nothing except the trouble of readjusting some of our less efficient industries.

But these less efficient industries have tremendous power in the lobby. They have great influence with Congressmen of both parties. For many years they have habitually contributed large sums to the campaign funds of both parties. They placed their bets, the proportion between the parties according to the probability of either party winning, but they played both sides, and so, I am told by reliable persons familiar with the procedure, they could not lose. Their very lives depend on governmental favor so they cannot perhaps be blamed for watching Washington so closely. They have been led by governmental policies of the past to feel that they have a vested right.

Previous to 1914, as I have said, the tariff policy of the United States may not have been altogether misguided, even though it enabled certain monopolies to profit unduly at the expense of the ordinary man. But since 1919 it has been obvious to all thinking people that sooner or later we must expose our inefficient industries to real competition from abroad, or else loan the centralizing power of government to our efficient industries, so that they can stop producing that which was formerly sold abroad.

As the tariffs are gradually reduced, may it not be wise to work out a plan for liquidating, definitely, yet slowly, these inefficient industries? It will be no more expensive to do this and no more troublesome to take care of the execu-

tive difficulties involved than it will be to retire indefinitely the fifty million surplus crop acres, the product of
which was so easily sold abroad in the old days when we
were a debtor nation.

One of the most interesting tariffs we ever had in the
United States was that of 1833 which provided for pro-
gressively reducing all tariffs that were above 20 per cent
ad valorem by a fixed percentage at stated intervals until
all of the tariffs were down to 20 per cent at the end of ten
years. In the United States today, tariffs are much higher
than they were a hundred years ago, but it might be wise
to consider reducing most tariffs which are above 50 per
cent by gradual steps to 50 per cent or below, or at least
downward toward 50 per cent to the fullest extent possible
under the Tariff Act of 1934.

Since the Tariff Act of 1934 provides for tariff reduction
only in consideration of reciprocal reductions abroad, it
would seem that a plan of this sort could only be carried
out as the result of a multilateral tariff arrangement. In
other words, a number of countries which have been hik-
ing their tariffs outrageously during the last seven or eight
years might go in with the United States on a pooled agreement. The farmers of England, France, Germany, Italy
and most of the rest of Western Europe would probably
object to an arrangement of this sort because it would
expose them to the more efficient wheat and pork production of the United States. It is my guess, however, that the
farmers of England and Western Europe would gain on
the whole by any such arrangement. The European price
of wheat, pork, and lard might go down but there would
be more employment in European factories and far more

prosperity among European dairy and market garden farmers. Of course, Western Europe in justice to her farmers, who have become accustomed to wheat at from $1.30 to $2.50 a bushel, would have to make the shift gradually, just as we would have to shift slowly in justice to those manufacturers who are producing types of goods which cannot, because of the situation, be produced efficiently in the United States.

If the President of the United States, using the tariff powers of 1934, can move forward slowly yet steadily toward reciprocal arrangements with other nations, and so make it possible for us to accept more of the goods which they produce most efficiently in exchange for the goods which we produce most efficiently, it may be possible within five or ten years to do away with much of the production control of the Agricultural Adjustment Act.

The old-fashioned, laissez-faire economists, especially those hooked up with the big banks, the boards of trade and the commission houses, are very enthusiastic about such possibilities. I agree with them in theory, but in practice I am wondering if it will be possible for the President to push his tariff bargaining so rapidly that foreign purchasing power will be sufficiently enlarged five or ten years hence to enable us to do away completely with agricultural control. Of course, I hope we can do away with much of it, but I fear, as I look at the nations which formerly took most of our agricultural products, that they may never again buy as much from us as they did before the war, during the war and immediately after the war.

I look at Germany and Italy which are now mature debtor nations, and realize that because of this fact, it is much more necessary for them now to grow a large percentage of their own food than they did before the war. Many of our former good customers now have the problem of learning to act as a debtor nation must act, just as we have the problem of learning to act as a creditor nation must act. A debtor nation must sooner or later export more than it imports, and the problem is to discover just which of goods formerly imported can now be produced at home.

The nature of the world's tariff problem can be illuminated by recalling some of the specific actions taken by foreign nations which have reduced the market for American farm products. Of course, in considering these, we must remember that the United States most unjustifiably led the way toward higher tariffs, beginning in 1922, and that much of the ensuing action on the part of foreign governments was retaliatory.

To stimulate increased production at home, Germany increased her tariff on wheat from $0.42 * per bushel in 1929 to $2.11 per bushel at the present time, on lard from $0.65 per hundred pounds to $18.10 per hundred pounds, and on leaf tobacco from $8.84 per hundred pounds to $32.58 per hundred pounds.

In addition, Germany instituted a system of quantitative restrictions on imports which has in some instances extended so far as to be almost an embargo. In 1929 Germany started wheat milling regulations which required German millers to use a high percentage of domestic wheat. In the crop year 1929-30 the percentage of domestic

* These figures on foreign tariffs are at the exchange rates prevailing on September 5, 1934.

wheat required to be milled was as high as 50 per cent, in 1930 as high as 80 per cent, and since 1932 further restrictions have been added. An import quota for lard was established in March, 1934, which restricted imports from the various sources of supply, chiefly the United States, to 40 per cent of the average annual imports during the three years 1931, 1932 and 1933. No lard was permitted entry into Germany from the United States beginning in July 1934. In the spring of 1934, Germany also introduced quantitative restrictions on the importations of cotton. This whole system of quantitative restrictions of imports has been backed by controlling the number of marks that might be converted into foreign currency for buying imports abroad.

Italy raised her tariff on wheat from 14 gold lira per hundred kilos ($0.74 per bushel) in 1929 to 75 paper lire per hundred kilos ($1.78 per bushel) at the present time and also introduced a system of required percentages of domestic wheat to be used in Italian mills similar to that of Germany.

France raised her duty on wheat from 50 francs per hundred kilos ($0.53 per bushel) in 1929 to 80 francs per hundred kilos ($1.46 per bushel) at the present time and, in addition, introduced a system of quantitative restrictions by means of import quotas unsurpassed for extensiveness by any other nation in the world.

England reduced the total quantity of cured pork imports from foreign countries and gave the United States 8 per cent of the reduced total. This means that during the present year, the United States may ship about 50 million pounds of cured pork, whereas in 1927 we shipped 164 million pounds and in 1921, 409 million pounds.

The wheat area in Western Europe, excluding Russia and the Danube Basin, increased from 46,900,000 acres in 1920 to 57,700,000 acres in 1933. The production increased from 777,000,000 bushels to 1,337,000,000 bushels.

The number of hogs in Germany and Denmark increased from 17 million head in 1921 to 30 million head in 1932.

I am not mentioning these developments to discourage people who believe in lower tariffs at home and abroad. My only purpose is to show in the light of facts that we may not be able to restore our old-fashioned agricultural market in foreign countries all at once.

Up to a certain point, I think good progress can be made. Many European nations are now beginning to realize that they have overplayed their hand; that by increasing the price of wheat to $1.50 or $2.00, or even more, they may have harmed their working population and their live-stock farmers far more than they have helped their wheat farmers. They are beginning to realize that expanding European agriculture means cutting down the market for European manufacturers abroad. It is possible that if the agricultural exporting nations use common sense, there may be some restoration of the customary trading of agriculture produce for manufactured goods. But while the customary channels of trade can be somewhat built up, it is possible that there will never be anything like a return to the pre-war situation. The hard fact is that so many of the nations of Europe are now in debt, and in the long run, debtor nations find it impossible to import goods as freely as creditor nations can.

For our part, it is obvious that the future outlines of our tariff policy should be developed in the light of the fact that we are now a mature creditor nation. We must now be prepared to accept more and more goods from abroad, or else forget the debts owed us from abroad. There is no reason why we cannot use the increased imports which foreign nations should be sending us to enhance the prosperity which we are striving for.

CHAPTER
VIII

AMERICA DISLIKES TO CHOOSE

For generations the American people have recognized that by manipulation of the tariff it is possible to go far in directing, restraining, stimulating, and balancing those forces which have to do with proportioning the national income. What seems to be overlooked now is that the tariff rules which worked fairly well in one economic situation may work poorly, or even disastrously, in a radically different economic situation. In the pinch of the present situation the only way out is to change the rules.

That is what the United States is trying—quite tentatively and hesitantly—to do today. I say "tentatively and hesitantly" because we are temporarily confronted by a choice of evils. It is not surprising that America dislikes to choose. But failure to choose can be disastrous. The 25 per cent of our people who live in the South and the some 15 per cent who live in the Middle West have been steadily bled and impoverished by buying in a protected market and selling on a world market.

I suppose the supreme trial of democracy is the ability to arrive at an intelligent decision under rapidly changing conditions with a fair degree of speed. No democracy has ever been exposed to such a terrific pressure as the United

States since 1919. At that time only about one person in ten thousand appreciated that the United States had become a creditor nation with a debtor nation psychology, and that there must be radical changes in American habits of thought, built up over several generations.

The greatest failure of American democracy in our time has been that involved in the inability of American political, academic, financial, and journalistic leadership of the United States to inform the voting public in terms of action, of the need of change. The leadership of America, instead of illuminating the truth so that all might understand, obscured it. During the period from 1920 to 1930 the people were led into easy-going acceptance of a belief that we could loan money abroad indefinitely.

The outstanding exception among the great men of the nation was Frank O. Lowden of Illinois. At Kansas City on June 7, 1922, one year after the Republicans had come into power, and at the time when the Fordney-McCumber Tariff Act was being considered, he had the courage and insight to say:

"You ask 'Is it not possible for America to recover this splendid isolation she has lost?' Yes, perhaps it is. The way is to let, say thirty per cent of our wheat fields go back into prairie and fifty per cent of our cotton fields go back into forests, and to close half of our copper mines and to curtail our production along many other lines. We can live within ourselves better perhaps than any other nation in the world if we are willing to pay the price, but we must readjust our whole life from one end to the other. I find no one who is willing to pay that price and therefore we have got to concern ourselves in the affairs of the world."

Thus Governor Lowden clearly analyzed the policies then being set in motion, and showed in them the seeds of ruin. The failure of the Republican Party to heed this warning, offered by one of the most loyal prairie-bred sons of the party, and its repudiation of Governor Lowden at the Kansas City convention in 1928, eventually led the party to impotence and intellectual bankruptcy, and brought the nation to its knees.

Not one person in ten thousand realized that the money which we invested so easily outside the United States during the period from 1920 to 1930 was building up an explosion that could shake the mightiest democracy of the world to its very foundation. By 1925 there were probably several thousand people in the United States who sensed the approach of tragedy, but none had any certainty regarding the time of the explosion. Some thought it might come as early as 1926 or 1927. Others thought we might go on loaning money abroad until 1940. The one thing they were sure about was that when the loaning abroad finally stopped, real trouble would be upon us. They could not guess just what accidental combination of circumstances would cause the fright which would interfere with the flow of funds into foreign investments.

Since 1930 we have had no surplus money to invest abroad, but the American people, in spite of their four long years of suffering, are still not ready to make the momentous decision their situation requires. The facts are increasingly well known. But the resolution to act in such a way as to make the whole economic picture add up to make sense is still somewhat remote.

More and more people are beginning to understand

that there is a relationship between the United States and the rest of the world which is in the nature of a double-entry bookkeeping or a balance sheet. If you change one side of the page there must inevitably be a change on the other side. If the United States should further build up her merchant marine and then pay foreign ships less for carrying American products, the result will be to cut down foreign purchasing power for our exports. If we insist on foreign nations paying us what they owe us at once, the result again must be reduced foreign purchasing power for our exports. The international balance sheet between the United States and the rest of the world, as expressed by imports of all kinds of goods and services on the one hand and exports of all kinds on the other, must add up to come out even. If it does not come out even the discrepancy must be made good by either short-time or long-time credit.

More than almost anything else, at present the different peoples of the world, and especially the American people need to understand the remorseless logic of international bookkeeping. When this logic is understood, it can then be realized that every policy, no matter what it may be, has its advantages and disadvantages. An increase in export trade must also be accompanied by an increase in import trade or by an increase in tourist expenditures in foreign countries, or by the shipment of more goods in foreign vessels, or by loaning money abroad, or by continually depreciating American currency, or by a little of any two or more of these five possibilities.

The United States is so wealthy in terms of intelligent people, great factories, rich soil, and scientific understanding, that she can for quite a period do nonsensical things, things which in almost any other nation would be immediately disastrous. More and more the nationalists and the internationalists in the United States are beginning to find fundamental facts. The nationalists are discovering that in case we go the whole route and insist on growing our own sugar, our own rubber, and eliminating all kinds of foreign imports as much as possible, it will be necessary to contract our export industries and agriculture by exceedingly resolute methods to a much smaller size. The extreme nationalists may not admit it, but it is probable that even a halfway nationalism such as is involved in maintaining the Hawley-Smoot Tariff schedule and loaning no more money abroad, means such a terrific slack in foreign purchasing power that the government for many years will have to step in and help the cotton farmers, the wheat farmers, the hog farmers and the tobacco farmers make multitudinous readjustments.

The honest high-tariff nationalists are more and more beginning to understand the price that must be paid. In its extreme form the price is regimentation, altogether repugnant to democratic traditions. But if education is properly carried out by an enlightened leadership in every community, the price might not perhaps be too great. Thus far, however, many of the nationalists seem to have been possessed with a kind of emotional fury which has made it difficult for them to understand the price a thorough-going nationalism demands. They have been propagandists for the advantages of nationalism and have dodged the disadvantages.

It is possible to be almost as critical of the internationalists. They speak in flowing terms of how increased imports into the United States will restore the normal market for our farm products abroad. They glory in the thought that we can get along entirely without any type of regimentation if the foreign markets are thus restored. But they do not like to indicate just which goods we are going to import. They talk glibly of non-competitive goods but find it difficult to point out just how much of what particular goods should be allowed to come into the United States.

Moreover, the internationalists are not as a rule familiar with the fact that there has been a tremendous expansion in European agriculture as a result of the subsidies of one kind or another which the European nations have given their farmers. How rapidly can European agriculture be contracted from its high point in the early '30s in order to reestablish markets for the exporting agricultural nations?

Personally, I have long favored a combination of the national and the international approach, but I recognize that this also has its peculiar difficulties. Such a course is hard to define with the necessary precision. In practice it means that the Agricultural Adjustment Administration would have to go ahead for a good many years keeping out of use perhaps 20 or 30 million acres of plow land, while the Presidential tariff powers of 1934 are being exercised as rapidly as is just and possible to restore a foreign demand for our surplus farm products.

Politically, the middle course is somewhat difficult. On the one hand it exposes the Administration to the criticism of those who do not like acreage control, and on the other hand to the criticism of those who do not like low tariffs. Logically, of course, a defender of high tariffs cannot object to acreage control under the post-war situation. But actually, the high tariff people, for hell-raising purposes, often disregard the logic of their position, defending high tariffs with one breath, attacking all efforts to adjust the international economy to the fact of high tariffs with the next.

I am convinced that if once the American people were fully informed of the facts of the post-war situation, and were willing to act accordingly, it would be possible for us rapidly to move into almost unimaginable prosperity. I am also convinced that if the nationalists and the internationalists continue to stalemate each other as they have ever since the World War ended, the result will be that the power of this marvelous country of ours will be checked and bound. We shall be continuously in a painful, convulsive, economic cramp, not unlike that which sometimes cripples the leg of a mighty athlete.

This is still a land of rare opportunity. What a vast body of well-educated people we are, situated in the midst of superabundant natural resources; but unfortunately since the World War, we have been baffled by such a complete change in our relationship with other nations, that we have been unable to make up our mind what to do.

Yet new forces are astir. During the past year several millions of our people have become hungry to get the facts and have studied them. We have not yet made up our minds, however; we seem not yet ready for manful action. If the President of the United States should strike out in decisive fashion toward a definite objective, would the

Congress and the people of the United States turn and rend him? Any President who understands the eventful necessities of this post-war situation must be gravely concerned with the changing understanding and the changing temper of the American people. He cannot get out too far in advance, but neither can he forget the educational duty of his position.

In my opinion many leaders in small towns and rural townships and some in great cities also, will eventually arouse public opinion to the point where the President and the Congress will find it possible to say, "America is going in this direction. We will pay the price and in so doing will lay the foundation for a prosperity far greater than that of 1929."

Yes, America dislikes to choose, but she will have to choose or she will eventually sink back into a situation worse than that of 1932. America can choose by using familiar democratic processes, even granting the dangers which harass these processes: deliberate lying, ignorance, prejudice, and that selfishness and hatred which seem to be so abroad in the land in a time of depression.

CHAPTER
IX

MONETARY POLICY

In THE leading nations of the world the monetary rules of recent years have been worked out by central banks, about half under the control of the government and half under the control of private banking institutions. The Federal Reserve System has been the U. S. version of a Central Bank.

Under the Constitution, it is the duty of Congress to coin money and regulate the value thereof; but from 1914 to 1933 Congress, in effect, turned this power over to the Federal Reserve System. The System established rules of the money game which on the whole pleased the bankers. Since 1933, the responsibility for establishing the rules of the money game has in very considerable measure been turned over to the President.

Money is a medium of exchange which serves as a symbol of confidence between nations and between people within the nations. When properly handled, money can be used to bridge both time and space. When properly working, it can be used satisfactorily to transfer labor of an American farmer in the year 1910 to a European laboring man in the year 1914, and vice versa.

Unfortunately, human judgment about the future, and about countries long distances away, is often bad. This was especially true during and after the Great War. But even under normal conditions, money is all too often handled to distort human judgment concerning the future. Money should—and can—be used to make possible a smoother transfer of goods from human being to human being, and from nation to nation, and to forward justice between the different classes of society.

Money troubles always begin during great wars. Governments invariably conclude that the older people who can not or do not go to war are so thoroughly selfish that the only way to get them to producing freely is to offer them exceedingly high prices. The demand for goods is great. The central banks acting under the direction of the government provide credit freely. The credit is manufactured on the basis of extensive issuance of government bonds which represent increased government debts. People get the idea during a long-drawn-out war that there is an unlimited demand at a high price for everything that can be produced. It is important to remember, however, that money manipulation during a war is responsible for only a part of the picture. Above everything else, there is a tremendous, genuine demand. The money manipulation in which the government is engaged merely makes this demand effective.

When a great war ends, the burden of debt is often so great that it is necessary to work out some definite scheme either for scaling down the debts or for cutting down the weight of gold behind the unit of currency. Since the close of the World War, practically every nation in the

world has used the second scheme and a few, notably
Australia, have used the first.

When a nation tries to lighten the burden of its internal
debts by raising the price of gold and reducing the number
of grains of gold in the unit of currency, the effect on
other nations is likely to be serious. When the French
increased the price of their gold in the middle twenties
until it was five times what it had been, they profoundly
affected the British. When the British increased the price
of their gold, they at once carried with them a large number of smaller countries and, after two and a half years,
the United States.

The price of gold in the United States today is $35 an
ounce as compared with $20.67 an ounce in early 1933.
The number of grains of gold in the dollar today is 14.28
as compared with 23.22 in early 1933. Many of the other
currencies of the world have slipped since early 1933, but
on the average foreign currencies in the fall of 1934 purchased about 45 per cent more dollars than in the early
spring of 1933. This means that, on the average, foreign
countries found it possible to buy about 45 per cent more
goods from the United States than in the spring of 1933
or else pay 45 per cent more, or a little of both. As a
matter of fact, the value of our total exports during this
period did increase by about 66 per cent.

President Roosevelt's monetary policy has undoubtedly
helped enormously the producers of those products which
are on the export market. France, at this writing, is paying about twice as much for cotton in terms of dollars
as she did in early 1933 but she is only paying about 20
per cent more in terms of French gold francs. For the

time being, therefore, the United States money policy has made it possible for both American exporters and importers of American goods to be happy. The exporters feel that they are getting a much higher price and the importers feel that the price is still remarkably reasonable.

All this, of course, is temporary money magic; it cannot last indefinitely. First one nation and then another can do this kind of thing and benefit from it temporarily. I am convinced that it was absolutely necessary for the United States to do something of the sort in 1933, unless we were prepared to go at it systematically to cut all debts, taxes and wages in half. We were not prepared to go that far so we took the only other safe course—controlled inflation. The President could still increase the price of gold from $35 an ounce to $41.34 an ounce, but he can't go further than that under the powers granted him by Congress.

There are many people who believe that if the price of gold is only high enough or if the Federal Reserve System only manages its credit sympathetically, there would be no need to worry about tariffs, production control, land planning, relief for the unemployed or any of the other things which have been tormenting us in recent years. Such people say: "Take care of money and everything else will take care of itself."

I think, myself, that the rules of the money game are exceedingly important, but I doubt if they are any more important than the rules of some of the other games. I see no possible way of handling the money question that will give foreign nations in the long run the same kind of purchasing power for our cotton, wheat, lard and tobacco

that they had before the war. We can create a temporary illusion that the situation is all right. We can do this
by loaning money to foreign nations for several years at a
time, or by increasing the price of gold and maintaining
the dollar at an artificially weak point by purchasing foreign currencies with our two-billion-dollar stabilization
fund. This last may work for several years, but it will not
work indefinitely.

Increasing the price of gold in 1933 got us off the hot
spot for a time. To the extent that it raised the international price level and lightened the burden of debt both
in this country and in foreign nations, it may get us off
the hot spot on to a warm spot. But raising the price of
gold in the United States will not serve permanently to
restore foreign purchasing power for our surplus farm
products. To solve that, we shall have either to import
more physical goods from abroad or else stop producing
so much for export. Nations can use money to deceive
themselves as to the location of their true markets for a
long time, but sooner or later the hard physical facts push
through.

The problem is to use money to guide us sensibly in our
production policy instead of to deceive us. During the
war, money was used to tell us the story of an endless
market at fantastic prices. After the war, money was again
used to deceive us as to the nature of the foreign market.
Loans were made to foreign nations at the time we were
raising our tariff, and the thoughtless ones who were interested only in markets tomorrow and next year, de-
ceived our people into thinking that we could go on in-

definitely expanding exports, raising tariffs, and collecting debts from abroad, without receiving goods.

In one way and another the money illusion has enabled fully 90 per cent of the people of the United States to avoid facing facts during 95 per cent of the time since the World War ended. During the war the money illusion was used as a sort of hypodermic to enable us to do certain things cheerfully even though they meant a headache later. Led on by the money illusion we did terrible things during the war; and since the war, we have been taking monetary headache powders of one kind and another continually. We still do not want to face fundamental facts.

But if you are really sick with a fundamental trouble, you must sooner or later admit it and act accordingly. You don't need to be downhearted about it. You can laugh and smile and face the facts resolutely. But there is always a time when you have to stop kidding yourself. It is difficult for any Administration to establish a fair, sound money policy unless the people themselves really understand and support it.

As a farm paper editor and later as Secretary of Agriculture, I have been especially interested in the rules of the money game. Farmers suffer more in a time of falling prices than any other class of people. They pay a higher percentage of their income in the form of such fixed charges as interest on debts, taxes, and freight rates.

During 1930, 1931 and 1932 the strongest move for increasing the price of gold and devaluing the dollar came from the organized farm groups. Throughout the twenties, a number of the influential, responsible farm groups felt that the Federal Reserve System should be specially directed to utilize its powers to stabilize the general price level at a point high enough to keep such fixed charges as interest on debts, taxes and railroad rates from being too great a burden. The Federal Reserve System thought that if this were done the result would be such an abundance of credit that production would outrun demand and there would be a wave of stock exchange and other speculation that would ruin the country.

During the early 1920's, under the influence of Governor Strong of the New York Federal Reserve Bank, the theory was developed that Federal Reserve Credit should be proportioned in such a way as to increase at the same rate as the physical quantity of goods. In other words, credit should increase at the rate of 3 or 4 per cent annually. Governor Strong thought that if credit were allowed to increase faster than this, the excess would be used to build factories, the products of which could not be sold to advantage. He thought that if credit were not allowed to expand this fast, there would be deflation, unemployment, falling prices and similar troubles.

As long as we have a capitalistic system, with the Federal Reserve Bank run on a half-and-half partnership basis of the government and private bankers, it seems to me that there is a lot of wisdom in Governor Strong's approach. He is dead now. His plan has never been given a fair trial. It still has a strong advocate, however, in Carl Snyder, statistician of the New York Federal Reserve Bank. But the expansion of credit at the rate of 3 or 4 per cent annually, excellent though it may be, is certainly not the sum total of banking or monetary wisdom. There are fundamental things especially wrong with world tariffs, exchange quotas, commodity quotas, and the like.

Some people say there should be neither money planning nor production planning of any kind. They would like to have the bankers and stock exchange people free to make their own rules in any way they see fit, so that the sucker public can furnish a recurring rich harvest. Others believe that there should be rules of the game governing tariffs, corporations, railroad rates, etc., but that the money rules should be left more or less open because they have no fundamental significance anyway. Still others believe that gold, silver and credit should be so handled as to bring about an expansion in usable money or credit at the rate of about 3 per cent annually. They feel that if this is done, there is little need for paying much attention to these rules of the game involved in tariffs, corporations, and the like.

For my part, I think we need new rules not only for money, but also tariffs, corporations, railroad rates, and a number of other things.

Later on, after the world begins to recover somewhat from the terrific shock given it during the World War and the economic warfare of the late twenties and early thirties, it may be possible to get rid of a good many of the rules.

Certainly we must not allow any monetary rules of the next five or ten years to bring upon us uncontrolled inflation. Some prices—not all—undoubtedly need to be higher than they have been thus far in this administration. But if we get them in a way which causes us to produce goods for a market which later doesn't exist, the result may finally be more painful than the situation of 1932.

We in the United States have never experienced the terrors of uncontrolled inflation with all the productive forces thrown out of balance because prices double every two or three weeks. Uncontrolled inflation comes like the breaking of the dam in the night and every one is swept along in the wildest confusion. All friends of economic justice will find their hearts' desires destroyed by the speculators if uncontrolled inflation comes to pass.

I have had some opportunity to watch the people who get behind inflationary movements. Many of them are disinterested. But I have also observed that most of those who put real money into an inflationary movement have a speculative axe to grind. In a time of inflation, those who are close to the government and can, therefore, guess the next move, can make short and rapid turns to their speculative profit. Farmers, with the possible exception of livestock traders, cannot make short, rapid turns; neither by temperament nor by the nature of their business are they fitted for the game. Farmers feel happy while the inflation is on. But the inflation always ends and the moment it ends the farmers are in worse trouble than anyone else.

In both city and country, uncontrolled inflation destroys the middle class, and thus points the way toward dictatorship.

So far as the farmer is concerned, his ideal situation would be to have a general price level considerably higher than at present, with a moderate assurance that after this level is reached, the dollar would remain fairly constant in purchasing power from one generation to the next. Of course, if the general price level continues to rise, the farmer has no assurance that his prices will rise as much as the prices of the things he has to buy. For that reason, the farmer is interested not only in money and credit as they affect the general price level, but also in those rules which have to do with the tariff and with production control measures to reduce the number of acres in this country that hitherto produced the surplus. Every time the farmer goes to the store he becomes less interested in the general price level, and more interested in the relation of farm prices to other prices. A balanced relationship between these prices cannot be maintained by monetary policy alone.

CHAPTER

X

COST OF PRODUCTION IN
AGRICULTURE AND INDUSTRY

ONCE the AAA and NRA were born, the price and production policies of all productive enterprise in the United States were thrust into headlines and limelight as never before. One proposed policy in particular drew attention. At times a guaranteed cost of production seemed in a fair way to be included as one of the new rules of the game. What happened in the farm sector is illustrative.

In April of 1933 John Simpson led the Farmers Union and Farm Holiday forces in a strenuous effort to get written into the Agricultural Adjustment Act the provision that farm products should be sold at a price representing cost of production. The cost of production for wheat was said, customarily, to be $1.40 per bushel, with other costs in proportion. The proponents of this method felt that the cost of production for farm products is best ascertained by discovering the price which would give farm labor a wage relatively as high as similarly skilled city labor, and farm investments a percentage return as high as that obtained by city investments.

According to Farmers Union leaders, this doctrine trans-
lated into 1932 prices on the farm, meant:

Corn	$ .93	per bushel
Wheat	1.37	per bushel
Oats	.50	per bushel
Hogs	11.42	per hundred pounds
Butterfat	.62	per pound
Eggs	.35	per dozen
Milk	2.74	per hundred pounds

—and other farm products in like proportion.

These prices were several times as high as in the spring
of 1933. The proposed cost of production amendment
conferred on the Government power of compulsory control of volume of marketing. Each farmer would be given
a quota. This he could sell at a designated time and place
at cost of production. The surplus he would either have to
store on the farm or sell on the foreign market.

I threw my influence against this plan in the spring of
1933, because I did not think the people of the United
States were ready for compulsory control of marketing,
and because the method of arriving at cost of production
was not defined in the Bill.

After the National Recovery Administration got into
action, many codes were adopted which provided for
price fixing, and some fixed prices at a point equivalent
to the cost of production. Of course, the farm groups which
had been turned down in their plea for cost of production
did not relish this. They said, "The farmer is just as much
entitled to cost of production as anyone else." They
pointed out that public utility rates and railroad rates
had been set on the basis of returning a certain wage to

the workers involved and a certain return on investment. The government made it possible for the railroads to hold up railroad rates to a point that railroads could pay their workers twice their pre-war wages. Why shouldn't the government hold up prices of farm products so that farm labor also could be paid twice what it got before the war?

The logic is irresistible, provided that farming can qualify as a public utility, and provided that farmers wish to submit to the public regulations which are imposed on the utilities.

The principle of "cost of production" is almost exactly that of "fair return." Both require, if there is to be government enforcement, a vast amount of government regulation and constant concern with books and profits.

For my own part, I have been getting more and more skeptical of the term "Cost of Production," whether it is used in agriculture or industry. Undoubtedly every individual should know his cost as accurately as possible. If he does not know it, he cannot know whether he is going ahead or falling behind. But the idea that cost can be used for either price-fixing or tariff-making, in either agriculture or industry, seems to me to be full of danger. No one has a divine right to cost of production. Moreover, cost of production is a false guide to prices over any long period of time. The true guide to prices is a concept based on that state of balance or ratios which make it possible for the economic organism to keep functioning with the least disturbance possible.

Cost of production looks too much toward the past. When an industry has been making large profits, it generally begins to pay its workers more and to spend money on improvements. In a new industry rapidly expanding, this may result in a decreasing cost of production. But after a time there is a tendency for cost of production to rise, simply because of the prosperity of the immediate past. In other words, if cost of production were recognized legally, there would be a tendency toward an ever-ascending spiral of prices raised by increasing overhead.

In illustration: the cost of producing a bushel of corn is made up chiefly of man labor, horse labor and the return on land. If the price has been good for several years, the cost of producing corn will be high. Horse labor will be high because the cost of horse labor is directly dependent on the price of grain and hay. Man labor and the land charge will be high; in the corn belt these are typically responsive to corn prices. If corn went to $2.00 a bushel, it would become possible to demonstrate that cost of production was $2.25 a bushel. Land would then be selling for ten times what it is today and farm labor would be getting two or three times as much. This tendency of cost of production to breed on itself makes it an exceedingly poor guide, from the standpoint of fixing prices, or balancing the national business structure.

It is wise for the individual business man and the individual farmer to hold up before his eyes the motto, "Know your costs." He must of necessity keep continually posted on his own individual competitive ability. But for government to take costs as a sole guide to price policies can easily prove exceedingly disastrous, especially if the cost of production policy is applied in different ways to different products. Furthermore, if cost of production were the prevailing policy for both farmers and business men, it is likely that business men would get the better of the farmer every time. It is so much easier to control industrial production than agricultural production.

Whenever the government or any business group undertakes to fix prices it should know what cost of production is, for both the most efficient and the average members of the group. But it should not seek in any very definite way to use cost of production prices as a guide.

The important thing, in cases where price-fixing is advisable, is to be sure about the type of control which can be exerted, over both production and marketing. The main question is: "Will the price set increase production, or marketing, or both, to a point where the control will break down? Will the price set reduce consumption, divert demand to other commodities and thus break down the control structure?" Often a price decidedly less than cost of production will bring about an over-production and a break-down in the control, simply because other competitive products are still lower in price.

For a commodity produced in one locality by a few thousand people, it is easy to fix prices and get away with it. Production and marketing control there can usually be air-tight; if the price goes down, supplies can be stopped. But when the government undertakes to fix prices for a great many commodities produced by millions of people, the problem becomes tremendously different. In the case of great commodities spread over wide areas of country, it is especially important to avoid arriving prematurely at any hard-and-fast idea about the proper price.

The fundamental concept is to get prices as rapidly as possible into such balance with each other that the different producers can live as happily as possible without getting into serious trouble later on. Perhaps this can be done by some form of group bargaining. We should be guided to a considerable extent by that ratio between prices which in the past has produced a relatively happy society. But we should be prepared to modify our ideas about the justice and workability of such ratios in the light of new inventions, new human desires, and new relationships between nations.

I am more and more convinced that when any industry is anxious to have government impose on it a price based on cost of production for its services, such industry should also be willing to accept governmental licensing and complete examination of books and records. Some parts of our economic structure have become like the hard wood in a tree, furnishing the central stiffness, no longer much interested in growth. It may be that these static portions of our economic life should be stabilized on some modified cost-of-production basis. Unfortunately, for this theory, the human social organism has thus far been growing much faster than any tree, and we have not been willing to accept even the railroads or electric light companies as permanent, static and, in the long run, absolutely essential elements in the economic structure.

The concept of cost of production, useful as it may be to the individual or to a particular class which is engaged in a campaign against other classes which are faring better, is decidedly tricky when it comes to formulating policies for shaping up the economic structure of the nation. There are perhaps several hundred thousand farmers who would like to strike for cost of production on their products in the same way that labor unions strike for a living wage. I do not care to criticize them for so doing. Such strikes may occasionally be politically useful and even economically useful under certain conditions; but fundamentally and eventually the whole doctrine of cost of production is unsound and should give way to the idea of that structure of balanced prices which will bring about a fair division between the different contributing classes, so that there will be the minimum of discord and upset.

I believe that the leaders of agriculture, labor, and business, in company with the representatives of the consumers, can gradually work out the principles on which would be based the ever-changing figures to carry out this principle of enduring balance.

CHAPTER
XI

SOME PRICES DON'T COME DOWN

IN PERIODS of inflation and deflation people become acutely aware of unfair price relationships, and begin to grope for remedies. They come to question the price rules of the game, and to ask who makes them, anyhow.

If the new world is to be genuinely different from the old world, our more adaptable, younger people must know a lot more about inflation and deflation, and the forces determining price, than my generation knew. Inflation and deflation sweep the world like storms, destroying homes and families. But they are man-made storms. They can be prevented to some extent if we are willing to shelter ourselves by adequate forethought.

Such storms break loose in all their fury only about once in a generation. I can remember my grandfather, in 1916, telling me of being offered 98 cents a bushel for barley in 1866. He held out for a dollar a bushel, saying that it would be easier to figure. Later he sold for 35 cents a bushel. At the time of the World War he saw the coming inflationary-deflationary storm and tried to get the information across to my generation. Probably a higher percentage of my generation anticipated the coming storm than had ever been true before. But it was not enough. The havoc wrought by the inflationary-deflationary forces in this particular period has been the worst in history.

The terrible thing about deflation, the thing that makes it cut so deep, and ruin so many lives, is that so many prices do not come down.

When deflation comes, prices fall in agriculture and in many industries, but in many other industries there is no corresponding fall. Instead, those who are in a position to dominate industrial policy maintain prices at their old level. As sales decline they reduce production. They throw men out of work and reduce the money income of the population. There is less income to spend. There is less demand—though not less need—for goods.

Some prices drop further than others. Economists call these flexible. Where prices are not flexible, however, less goods are sold; then less goods are produced, and more people become unemployed. This is true whether the inflexible prices are set by the government, as in the postal service; through governmental commissions, as in railroad and utility rates; or by private enterprises, as in the case of aluminum, agricultural implements, and many paint products.

To these inflexibilities in price must be added inflexible charges from debts and taxes. By staying high they further exaggerate the shrinkage in the amount of goods that can be bought with a reduced income. Such changes, following an inflationary period, can come with breath-taking speed, destroying the incomes of all groups—the farmers, because farm prices are so low; the workers, because so many are unemployed; the owners of factories, because the factories are so inactive; the owners of securities and the banking system, because basic economic values have been destroyed by low incomes and inaction. All these rigidities and disparities in the prices of goods and services make for a multitude of injustices, ever deeper depressions, heavier drags on recovery.

These are economic convulsions and cramps which flow from deflation following a great war. Perhaps I have put it too abstractly. Let the reader, then, picture in his mind a father or brother or cousin who was well-to-do in 1920 but who is now nearly penniless. What did he do that was wrong? Probably his mistake was to guess that certain prices would stay up, or that if the fall came, all prices would come down together. He did not fully appreciate that some prices and charges come down very slowly, if at all. He did not know that the price structure we have let grow here is half of steel and half of putty.

The debt price does not come down; therefore the people who loaned money when commodity prices were high can cause great grief to borrowers when commodity prices crash. They have a legal right to ask for the fulfillment of their contract. This causes much property to change hands. Those who control the big industries, in their efforts to protect themselves and their stockholders, throw most of the burden of depression on the wage workers whose purchasing power is wiped out by unemployment. Prices of some goods and services are held up in the hope that somehow a larger volume of business will soon be forthcoming and profits at those relatively high prices restored. Much political ferment and economic and social legislation in a depression period springs out of the fact that some prices come down and others do not.

During the deflation following a great war, prices of certain products go almost to the vanishing point. This is particularly true of the products that have an international market. Wheat, corn and rye, for example, nearly trebled their pre-war values in 1919, but by the summer of 1932 had lost eighty to ninety per cent of their wartime peaks and had fallen to less than a third of their pre-war values. At the same time, farm debts per acre, built upon the inflated prices, were nearly three times as high as before the war. Taxes were more than twice as high.

Under such circumstances, lending institutions, pressed by their own obligations to depositors, stockholders, or to insurance policy holders, feel that they must have payment of principal and interest on debts; local governments needing revenue feel they cannot permit tax delinquency. Over vast rural areas many families, after a lifetime of honest toil, face foreclosure,—homeless, hopeless.

Debts and taxes are not the only rigid prices which lead to the blind reshuffling of the wealth and income of the nation during periods of deflation and depression. Prices of goods and services that are used in production and that enter into the average consumer's budget, the fees of doctors and lawyers, and the commissions charged by dealers, telephone, electric light, and railway charges, and even wage rates in organized industries, remain much higher than they were before the war.

When farmers see prices of their products fall to a half or less of what they were before the war, and find trans-

portation rates remaining about 50 per cent above their
pre-war rates; when they see farm machinery prices practically unchanged at about 50 per cent above their pre-war
levels, building material prices 30 per cent above pre-war,
and prices of fertilizer, equipment and supplies at pre-war
levels or higher, they feel tremendously abused. Some of
their products have an exchange value for certain industrial products of only one-third or perhaps only one-fifth
or one-tenth of that before the war. They know that something is wrong, that something must be done, for if nothing
is done, they know that they will sink.

The city wage-worker likewise finds himself caught between a reduced or vanished income and prices that do
not come down or that come down only part way. In the
first phase of post-war deflation, during 1920-22, city living
costs came down about 15 per cent. Workers who were
fired or whose hours and wages were cut more than 15 per
cent were much in the position of the distressed farmer,
especially if the wage-worker had, like the farmer, committed himself to a mortgage on a home or to some other
inflated obligation.

Fortunately for the average wage earner, the industrial
recovery of 1923 restored his earnings. In the second
phase of post-war deflation, that after 1929, city living
costs in general again came down haltingly. Some costs
did not come down at all. The real burden of the faulty
economic and social decisions arising out of the war and
post-war policies is being borne by the ten million people
still unemployed in 1934 and by the farmers with unwar-
rantedly low incomes. Their meager savings, if any, might
go farther in keeping body and soul together if living

costs in general had declined more than the 25 per cent decline that did take place, and if the costs of fuel, doctor care, education, and transportation had been less rigid.

Inflexibilities in retail prices squeeze the farmer and the laborer at the same time. When powerful distributors maintain such charges as freight rates, labor rates, or commission and profit rates, they prevent retail prices from falling to points within reach of the city man's reduced earnings, and they force down the farmers' share of the consumers' dollar.

Business men who use the power concentrated in their hands to control output and to keep their prices relatively high, are not alone in their shortsightedness. Often the wage policies of organized labor in periods of depression are just as shortsighted.

Labor unions after the war succeeded in maintaining wage rates about twice as high as before the war. Much of this gain was undoubtedly justified: in some industries there had been sweatshops to fight. But the efforts of labor to hold on to high nominal wage rates during the depression, even though that policy meant going without work, intensified and prolonged the depression in exactly the same way as the manufacturers' efforts to hold on to relatively high nominal prices with factories largely shut down.

Each group, by insisting on inflexible prices for wages and commodities, lowers the purchasing power of groups whose prices and incomes are flexible. Price rigidities of this sort prevent that resumption of activity in steel, lumber, and other capital goods industries which has usually helped get us out of depressions. More sensible wage and price policies, especially in capital goods industries, would put pay envelopes in the hands of millions of unemployed, and would have brought a quicker revival in our most essential industries.

The money-minds, so-called, and the directors of public utilities, demonstrate still another form of rigidity during the deflation which follows a great war. They would hold on, at any cost, to the advantage to which they believe their contracts entitle them. Debtors, especially farmers, are convinced that these groups cannot, in the long run, collect in full, no matter what the law may be; that, unlike Moses, these groups cannot draw water out of a stone. There follows a time of great political confusion, during which the politicians pass laws to make the monied and public utility groups see the economic truth of the debtors' situation.

These laws take two forms. They try to raise the price of the products sold by the great farming and manufacturing classes, and they endeavor to write down obligations and reduce property taxes.

History over many centuries is strewn with price-raising and debt-reducing efforts as one nation after another has had to face the aftermath of wartime inflation. But no matter how energetic and radical the laws may be, the net result is to perpetuate a large part of the maldistribution of national income. In the United States since the World War, the percentage of the national income going to creditor and public utility classes has been greatly increased, and the percentage going to farmers has been greatly reduced.

Before the war, our farmers received about 15 per cent of the national income. In 1932 they received about 7 per cent. Part of this decline in the share going to agriculture is due to the expansion in urban population, but even on a per capita basis farmers have lost out. Before the war, the farm population—30 per cent of the total— received 15 per cent of the total national income; at the bottom of deflation in 1933, the farm population, now 25 per cent of the total, received only 7 per cent of the national income. The income per person gainfully occupied in non-agricultural pursuits before the war was about $700, and the income per person gainfully occupied in farming was about $475, or about two-thirds of what others were earning.

During the brief period of wartime inflation, farmers received a larger share of the national income and the individual earnings in industry and agriculture were more nearly in balance, but that gain was more than wiped out by the first period of post-war deflation in 1920-22. In the fat years of 1925-1929, with little unemployment in the land, non-farmers were earning about $1500 a year; the average farmer, not much more than half as much. In 1932 the 25 million people who had jobs were earning a little less than $1300 a year; the 13 millions who had no jobs were living on charity or savings; while farmers earned about $400 apiece, a good part of which was in the form of food and fuel they raised themselves, not cash with which to pay the expenses of running a 150-acre farm business, and keeping and providing for the needs of a family of five.

Those at the other end of the economic scale, remote from "busted" farmers and unemployed wage-earners, are the privileged few whose very high salaries remain high even during such a severe deflation and depression as that of 1932, and those who receive their incomes as interest payments on long-term debts. While there is some defaulting of interest, deflation touches the flow of interest payments last of all. They continued to expand well into 1930, a year after the present depression set in, and in 1932 still totalled 5.9 billion dollars, or 12 per cent of the national income, compared with 6.2 billion or 7.5 per cent of the national income in 1929. Dividend payments did not shrink materially until the second year of the depression. By 1932, dividend payments were only 5 per cent of the national income as against 7 per cent in 1929.

The industries that are sheltered during deflation by rates and charges fixed by governmental bodies, fare unusually well. Not only did public utilities as a group receive a larger share of the national income after the war, but they have managed to increase that share somewhat since 1929. In that year, the incomes of these industries amounted to 10.9 per cent of the total; in 1932, 12.3 per cent. This relatively favorable situation is also reflected in the welfare of those whose incomes come from interest payments on the bonds of public utilities. In 1929 these interest payments amounted to more than a billion dollars; in 1932, to nearly 1.2 billion dollars. Even though there may have been some increase in the number of bondholders, the relatively favorable condition of the groups attached to or dependent upon these industries protected by government rate-fixing commissions is obvious.

It would seem the part of wisdom for creditors and the owners of public utilities to do everything possible to restore purchasing power to farmers and other debtors. Thus the insurance company executives who worked with farm leaders during 1931 and 1932 on the domestic allotment plan were looking beyond the ends of their noses. They realized that if farm product prices were not restored, some farmers of necessity would have to repudiate some of their debts, and that in the process they might get a certain amount of government help.

This analysis is not presented to arouse prejudice between different groups, but merely to awaken thought. The burden of the prices and charges which have not come down is still great. There will be further reductions in many of them unless farm product prices advance even faster and farther than they have thus far.

Where a frontal attack on rigid prices is not feasible, a flank attack may do as well. Consider, for example, the competitive situation between railroad rates, organized truck rates, and disorganized farmer truck rates. Railroad rates are theoretically based on wages twice the pre-war rate and an investment greater than the pre-war. Organized truck rates are based on wages at 40 cents an hour or better. But farmers own their trucks to do their own hauling. Many farm truck owners are happy to haul on the basis of their own labor at 10 or 15 cents an hour. The prices for their farm products have all too often returned them, for their labor, less than 5 cents an hour. The farm

trucker is a small but continuous menace to the organized trucker and the railroad freight rate structure.

Those who would legislate or codify the farm trucker
out of business should think twice and then again. In many
different ways low farm product prices and the cheap farm
labor flowing therefrom will sooner or later menace all
of the artificially high city services. Legislation and codes
will furnish the unduly high city services only temporary
protection. Attempts to maintain such protection will after
a time cause great bitterness on the part of those who have
been ground down to the bottom of the heap and are denied what seems to them a profitable outlet for their labor.
Enduring protection will come only when all the prices
and wages in question are in a workable relationship
with each other. Until such relationship is established,
codes and legislation are mere stop-gaps.

Our modern price structure, I have said, is half of steel
and half of putty. The reasons lie deep in the nature of the
business world that has grown about us.

The whole character of economic organization has
shifted within the last century. A hundred years ago most
activity was carried on by individuals or very small enterprises. This individualistic activity was largely organized
and coordinated through the buying and selling that took
place in the market-place. The market-place, that is, was
the automatic control of our economic system. The whole
economy operated on principles similar to those which
have affected agriculture to our own day.

Thus, in agriculture we now have six and one-half million separate farmers. Before 1933 these six and one-half

million farmers were each attempting to conduct their business in the light of their own experience and necessarily limited knowledge of general supply and demand. Few were aware of the forces which determine whether they get a good or a meager return for their year's labor. Low prices—whether from excessive acreage, or bumper yields, or bountiful crops abroad, or industrial unemployment—cause the individual farmer to shift from one crop to another or from crops to livestock production. But low prices or high prices, he cannot let his 160 acres and his own labor be idle. He considers that producing something is better than producing nothing at all. The result is that for the country as a whole the total acreage in harvested crops remains practically constant from season to season. Six and one-half million individual farmers have no control of production, and no control over the markets.

Nor do the millions of ultimate consumers of farm products have any control over production or price. Rather, the control of production and price lies with the market itself, as it registers the interacting pressures of producer and consumer. Each individual acts in his own interest. The conflict of interest brings production and prices for each product which represents neither sole control by producers nor sole control by consumers. The farmer who shifts from the production of pork to the production of milk, because of higher prices for milk, is acting according to the interests of consumers. The higher price means that consumers want more milk produced. At the same time, obviously, the farmer is attempting to serve his own immediate interest. In this way the free market and flexible prices tend to work out a balance between the interests of

individuals as producers and the interests of individuals
as consumers.

When practically the whole economy operated on the
basis of the free market and flexible prices, as it did a century ago, not only farming but all other kinds of businesses
were after a fashion coordinated by the market. The interests of individuals producing in one industry were balanced against the interests of individuals consuming the
products of that industry though perhaps holding the role
of producer in another industry. Under such a system conflicting economic interests were brought to a balance
through the market. Control of industrial and agricultural
policy—of prices and production—lay in the impersonal
hands of the market and not in the hands of any single
group of people.

When industry began to grow from the one-man shop
into the factory, the influence of the market-place began
to suffer. No longer was it the arena where producer met
consumer on a completely individualistic basis. The shoes
for sale in the market were not now the product of John
Jones, fashioned as he himself thought best, sold at a price
and time he thought wisest. Rather, they were the product
of many John Joneses, working under the direction of a
boss. The boss, not the primary producers, made contact
with customers, with other producers, and with the market-
place. The boss, not the primary producers, decided what
to make, how to make it, when to sell, how much to sell,
and at what price to sell it.

To be sure, it is this specialization and this administrative coordination which, combined with machinery and
power, makes factory enterprise so effective. But the shift

from coordination by the market to coordination by the boss reduces by so much the area of control left to the market. This in itself would be unimportant so long as the individual enterprises remained small and numerous. But the last hundred years have seen a gradual concentration of industrial activity into bigger and bigger units, a concentration that has gone on at a rapidly accelerated pace during and since the World War, and has reached the point where 200 great enterprises in the United States now control over half the industrial wealth and approximately half the industrial jobs in the country. Tremendous chunks of economic activity, consequently, have been taken out of the area of market coordination and put into the hands of private business administration. In 1929, for example, the American Telephone and Telegraph Company alone was coordinating the activity of over 400,000 employees. The Great Atlantic and Pacific Tea Company had 15,000 separate stores and sold more than a tenth of all the groceries sold at retail in the United States. Does the free market-place of a century ago exist for them?

Certainly these developments have brought increased technical efficiency. It is largely because we have these great organizations that we can envisage that economy of plenty which the technicians promise us if only we can solve the problem of getting what the technicians can produce into the hands of consumers.

But the shift from market-place to private administration has meant that to a very significant extent industrial policy-making has likewise shifted from market control to control by individuals. By the process of concentration more and more threads of control over industrial policy were drawn into the hands of business men managing our great corporations. In some instances certain threads of control were carried through to governmental commissions; this was true of railroad rates.

To just the extent that the control of industrial policy was shifted from the market-place to administrative hands, the share in control which the workers and consumers including farmers had formerly exercised over industrial policy *through the market* was reduced, and the powers of business management (or commission) were increased.

What has been the effect of this shift? The market-place of 1834 produced an industrial policy which represented a rough balance between various economic interests; in 1934 the industrial policies established by the corporate managements in our more concentrated but unregulated industries do not represent such a balance. Quite properly under the existing rules of the business game, the business managers produce at a price and a volume which they hope will maximize profits or minimize losses. As a result, industrial policies involving prices and production are established primarily in the interests of business groups. Because so little control over the essential elements of industrial policy remains with the market, the decisions made all too frequently interfere with the effective functioning of our economic machine.

Thus during a depression it is frequently in the immediate business interest of a large enterprise which has effective control over price and production policy to choose to hold prices at their old levels and to curtail production rather than to continue production at a higher level and accept a lower price as farmers do. This does not mean that they make unreasonable profits—even by this policy, they may suffer losses.

We may be sure that if consumers were to determine price and production policy for such an industry, they would maintain production and lower prices up to the point that would still allow the financial survival of the enterprise. A wage, price, and production policy determined by labor might fall between these extremes. Labor would want to see maintained a volume of production which would allow sales to the consumer at a unit price sufficient to yield a good wage, and allow the enterprise to continue in business.

Note the result of these three different policies. Industrial policy-making by business men in the interest of profits would, during deflation, make the adjustment to changed demand by lowering production and maintaining price. (The railroads even asked the ICC for permission to raise rates because volume of traffic had fallen so greatly.) This means increased unemployment and a further drop in demand, hurrying our whole economy into further distress. In such case the business enterprises are producing very much less than they would be *willing* to produce and sell at the price they are maintaining. Supply and demand would not be made equal by price, but rather production and demand would be made equal *at* a price.

On the other hand, a policy determined by consumers would keep the producing facilities, both men and machines, going full tilt as far as financial resources would allow. The product would be sold for what it would bring, much as the market mechanism has forced the farmer to do. But such a policy might easily deplete the capital equipment of industry to a point where further production would be impossible without high costs. The same would be true if farmers set the industrial policy for the agricultural implements industry. Such policies would make for full employment but might easily result in insufficient capital equipment. And if industrial policy were set by labor, it is likely that nearly full production and employment would be maintained but there would again be a danger of depleting the capital equipment.

The effect of business control of industrial policy is clearly indicated during the depression. Between the first quarter of 1929 and the first quarter of 1933, when agricultural production had changed practically not at all, and prices had fallen more than 60 per cent, industrial productions had been cut in two, building activity reduced by 90 per cent, and thousands of individual enterprises were completely shut down. The farmer faced the problem of selling in a domestic market where thirteen million people were unemployed. Industrial prices in general had declined less than half as much as agricultural prices; a number of them remained practically unchanged. At the low point of 1933 farm prices averaged 60 per cent lower than in 1926, textiles 49 per cent, food prices 47 per cent lower, hides and leather 32 per cent lower, building materials 30 per cent, metals, chemicals and house furnishings about 29 per cent, and metal products 23 per cent lower. During this interval, prices of metals and metal products had declined only about two-fifths as much as had agricultural prices. In general, the greatest decline occurred in unconcentrated raw materials; prices of manufactured goods declined only a little. Agricultural prices fell farther than non-agricultural, and prices of goods destined for eventual consumption declined more than prices of goods used in capital equipment, such as building materials and machinery.

These price inequalities mean, of course, that producers of goods bringing relatively low prices cannot buy the relatively high-priced products. Industries maintaining relatively high prices, with their workers largely unemployed, have no added purchasing power as a result of their price advantage. Even if the few owners of those industries have some temporary advantage because their products have a purchasing power larger than that of other commodities, their contribution to recovery is certainly nil. Surely it is more important to the nation as a whole that the purchasing power of farm products be kept relatively high, so that six and one-half million farmers can buy more abundantly of building materials, and farm equipment, and automobiles, and other industrial products, thus supporting employment, than that the purchasing power of a few business men be kept high. They are few in number; their consumption of food and clothing is limited.

I do not mean this in a personal sense. The reluctance of business men to lower prices during a depression must not be too strongly held against them. They have acted according to the rules of the game as they have been handed down to them from the days when industrial policies were so largely determined by a market which balanced the interests of buyer and seller, of worker, farmer, business man, and consumer.

But now that conditions have changed, now that so

much of industrial policy has been taken out of the market—and I believe that modern technology and an economy of plenty demand this—we can well hold it against business men who fail to see that it is necessary to change the rules of the game. Indeed, it seems probable that if in the last three years industrial policies had been formulated to balance the interests involved, the losses of business men during the depression would have been vastly less or would have been converted into real profits.

To the extent that further control over industrial policy is taken out of the market-place by abrogating the anti-trust laws, there is every reason why such newly created powers should be lodged in bodies such as code authorities or control committees which are truly representative of the various economic interests. Particularly is it important that any powers of control over prices, production, or new investment should not be lodged primarily in the hands of those who are trying to increase money incomes of special groups—which can so often be done as easily by creating scarcity as by creating plenty. Only as such industrial policy is determined to bring a balance between business men, workers, farmers, and consumers, will the result be in the public interest. Only then will the optimum volume of goods and services be forthcoming at prices which will take them off the market yet yield fair wages and a return on capital sufficient to maintain capital equipment and to permit such additions as progress demands.

One of our major problems is to set up such conditions that, where industrial policy can no longer be effectively controlled by the market, other mechanisms will bring a balanced result. For the balanced operation of our economic machine, labor and consumer must be built into the structure of industry. Here lies a great challenge to the new frontiersman. Can labor, and particularly the consumer, effectively share in the making of industrial policy? Without them, and particularly without the consumer, whether he be the worker spending his income or the farmer buying supplies or machinery, we shall continue to have industrial policy made to create profits at the expense of abundance. Only industrial policy made largely in the interests of consumers will bring us an economy of plenty.

A hundred years ago Americans did not have these problems. Even then, to be sure, a wartime inflation and post-war deflation did distort men's judgments on prices, but the distortion was not so serious; automatic correctives were quick and sure. Today the differential rigidities of a deflation are exceedingly serious. Whole classes and groups, profiting enormously at the expense of other classes and groups, do not realize what an economic injustice they are committing. They think they are merely enjoying their liberty. The economic and political strains thus created are quite as likely to end in demagoguery as in constructive action.

Groups striving against each other with purposes narrow and selfish, will produce mutual destruction. They must learn to think of the problem as a whole. The demagoguery of the debtor group has been no worse than the ignorance of a creditor group which would not and could not understand. New rules of this game cannot, in all justice, be decided solely by those whose interest lies in the prices which do not come down.

CHAPTER
XII

MILLIONAIRES, BOOMS, CHAOS

AFTER 1929, it ought not to be necessary to say that we shall never advance to our new world on the crest of a speculative boom. In boom-time there is no thought of changing the fundamental rules of the game. The flimsy superficialities of each hectic moment are in command. What is done with tariffs or with price and production policies does not appear to matter.

With this view of speculative sprees I think most men would agree today. But will they agree five or ten years hence? Will those who were youngsters in 1929, and who, in a few years, will be in the saddle be capable of profiting by our experiences? Will they keep their eyes on fundamental rules, even in times of greater prosperity?

Unfortunately, the youth of one generation fail, as a rule, to profit by the experiences of the youth of the preceding generation. Again and again this country has gone through a speculative jag, each followed by a depression worse than the one before. Little did the aspiring millionaires of 1928-29 know or wish to know of sad experiences buried with get-rich-quick schemers of the past. They found the game exciting; the "New Era" theory of everlasting prosperity had been well drilled in; and the ease with which, between 1925 to 1929, many stepped into the millionaire class made the pursuit of a quiet profession or a moderate way of life exceedingly old-fashioned.

The mistakes we made after the war, the way we handled our foreign trade, our credit system, our farm production, would not have let us in for half the misery if there had not been reared upon those mistakes the colossal speculative boom. Millions of us were swept out of our normal pursuits to follow the exhilarating dance of the stock market or the real estate market.

Our readiness to continue lending abroad during 1920-1923 helped shorten the life of the industrial depression of that period, but farmers continued to press the product of their wartime acres on the foreign markets where they were no longer needed. While this served to prolong the farm depression, the city man with food costs relatively low and employment expanding, enjoyed a larger share of the national income.

The building industry revived to make up for homes not built during our preoccupation with the war. The automobile industry received another boost and the radio and airplane industries were expanded rapidly. Our preference for European gold in place of foreign goods as payment for the debts owed to us brought an inflow of gold and paved the way toward the 1929 boom. It did so because an abundance of credit at low interest rates grew out of the ample gold supplies and this made for further industrial expansion, rising stock prices and easy-money-making opportunities.

The small world wheat crop in 1924 made great profits

for wheat speculators. Prices bounded from less than $1.00 per bushel to over $2.00, and we had a few more millionaires at the expense of the usual large number of "lambs." By 1925 we were well along the exciting road that eventually led to destruction. Promoters began to spread their enticements far and wide into town and hamlet. More and more of us joined the procession. In the industrial booms of 1919 and 1923 we had managed pretty well with no more than 75 persons with yearly incomes of a million dollars. By 1925 we had nearly three times as many.

Under these stimulating circumstances, domestic corporations found it easy to sell new securities to the unwary. Building activity was lifted to a dizzy level. Ready credit and the pursuit of millions led to the crazy competition in taller and taller skyscrapers. The automobile industry expanded enormously on the basis of "a dollar down and pay the rest as you can." State and local governments went into debt to provide good roads, and the automobile industry was further aided in the export field by our readiness to lend abroad. Thus we built to the limit one industry after another.

The speculative mood was upon us. We saw security values rise higher and higher under direction of men in control of wealth. Making money seemed easy. All we needed was faith in the continued prosperity of the country. The old slogan, "Never Sell America Short," was revived; young men then entering business were given the solemn injunction to seek lucrative opportunities in private pursuits and to avoid the clammy hand of bureaucracy. It was considered silly to go into public office when brains were so handsomely rewarded in industry, commerce and speculation. Many a youth, to his later sorrow, found it easy to accept this attitude, for the number of successful business men was growing apace. By 1928-1929 we had ten times as many million-a-year men as in the period 1919-1923. To the young, these stood as shrewd, successful business men, when as a matter of fact, they were merely riding a wave shakily supported by forces they did not understand.

It is said that more brains have been wastefully put into the pursuit of easy stock market profits than into any other single American enterprise. What a pity that the business youth of the country and the maturer business men could not have been directed to use their physical and mental vigor in an effort to promote a balanced industrial economy, instead of squandering themselves on trying to outguess the other fellow. What we needed in 1925 was not more millionaires, but a way of directing a larger share of the national purchasing power into rural areas to balance agricultural with industrial progress. We needed a transfer of some of the business geniuses from their excessive concern over taller skyscrapers to an interest in rural rehabilitation. More purchasing power in the country, and an effort to raise the farmers' standard of physical surroundings, might have prevented the excessive over-building in the cities. We would not have had such a complete collapse in a major industry, the revival of which is so essential to general prosperity.

I am not so much concerned with the number of millionaires and the size of their individual wealth as I am with their power. They have enormous power to influence the minds and aspirations of the young, and to shape or misshape our progress. I am concerned over the power that heretofore we have placed in the hands of the large-salaried executives and the large stockholders to determine the kind of progress we are to have. The toll the distributor, or manufacturer, or banker takes out of the dollar of millions of consumers to build his fortune may be small, but with this privilege of collecting a little from millions there has also been exercised a power over legislation, over farm programs, over the course of industrial activity that often has done the country a great deal of harm.

Consider the fact, previously stated, that two hundred of our larger corporations control through their managers the jobs of something like half of the industrial employees of the country; and you can easily imagine the economic and social chaos which would ensue if these few industrial leaders and managers, in a moment of fear, were all to turn their backs on the common good in order to preserve property earnings and high salaries. Out of this power that goes with the privilege of great wealth, springs many of our difficulties in launching programs for the benefit of distressed farmers, laborers and merchants, and many delays in the New Deal are traceable to this misused power.

The possession of wealth is not an iniquity. We have many millionaires who have used their wealth as a public trust, to be redistributed for the benefit of all. But when wealth is used to rig markets; when the infectious success of one manipulator stirs the envious hopes of a multitude of the rising business generation; when the heedless, narrow-visioned actions of these misguided ones then spread their influence over the populace until millions are engaged in a speculative mad-house, such as we lived in in

1928 and 1929; when our daily speech in the East begins and ends with the price of "U. S. Steel Common," and in the West with "Bank of Italy Common," to the exclusion of the fundamental things in life, then we have chaos and calamity.

Instead of the intelligent manipulation of forces for the general welfare, we had a great striving for individual accumulation. Instead of an equitable distribution of the product of industries, we had the growth of cash reserves and surpluses in the hands of stockholders who used them to fan the fires of speculation. Instead of a coordinated advance in all sections of industry and agriculture that might have made for stability, we had distortions that clogged our industrial blood. The building industry had over-reached itself in 1925; the automobile industry had over-reached itself in 1928; the wheat farmers were piling up surpluses that kept them poor. But none of these mad, unbalanced situations was visible to eyes glued on daily advances in the speculative markets. Truly it is madness, when the writing-up of paper values is taken for real substance.

The financial gods we worshipped before the 1929 crash have disappeared. They fell with the collapse of the fantastic financial structures they built out of the swapping of dollars and paper certificates. Perhaps we needed that experience so that our sense for the truer gods and values beyond present frontiers may now receive our wholehearted allegiance.

THIRD SECTION

THE AGRARIAN DRIVE TO CHANGE THE RULES

INTRODUCTION

Farmers have probably been more active than any other group in searching for economic democracy. This is not because they are any more intelligent, any more virtuous or any more courageous than the people of other classes, but because they have suffered more, and because they still live in the simpler and plainer environment wherein this democracy was born.

When changed conditions took away what they considered to be their rights they decided to fight. In fighting they followed the traditional methods of democracy. Year after year they have continued their fight and year after year they have learned new lessons.

Slowly, almost grudgingly, the high-tariff farmers of the Middle West learned that the fundamental object of the tariff was to help manufacturers, not farmers. For twelve long years they tried to get the equivalent of a tariff for agriculture. At first the farmers were as selfish and narrow-minded in their approach as any small business group or labor union. But as the agricultural movement assumed national proportions, internal debate between leaders of

West and South, North and East, developed a much greater breadth of concept.

In their efforts to obtain a fair share of the national income the farmers at one time and another from 1921 to 1932 attacked or adopted nearly all the rules of the game available in a democracy. They tried their hands on tariffs, export subsidies, monetary policies, railroad freight rates, new methods of taxation and a great many other levers. They were not guided by any philosophy or doctrine. Their sole objective was a fair share in the national income, or as some of them put it, "Cost of production plus a reasonable profit."

The next four chapters describe how farmers attempted to modify the rules of the game in the interests of justice. Narrow-visioned as many of the farm leaders may have been when this fight was first started, I am convinced that as stormy years went by, they have, in considerable measure, educated not only themselves but their followers and the people in the cities. The job is by no means completed, but the process has been so illuminating that I am setting it down here in some detail.

The experimental method of democracy may be slow, but it has the advantage of being sure. When you change people's minds you change the course of a nation.

Though abundance is at hand, we still live by old standards of denial. The situation is confusing. There are those who say that there cannot be a surplus so long as there is a single hungry Chinaman. Fundamentally and eventually this may be true; but these standpat sentimentalists who weep that farmers should practice controlled production do not suggest that clothing factories go on producing *ad*

infinitum, regardless of effective demand for their mer-
chandise, until every naked Chinaman is clad. Nor do
they feel that plow factories should abandon production
control until every hungry Chinaman has a plow. We must
play with the cards that are dealt. Agriculture cannot survive in a capitalistic society as a philanthropic enterprise.
If the cry of those who bid our farmers think of all those
hungry Chinamen, and plant more land, were heeded, it
would mean that long before the last hungry Chinamen
were taken care of, hundreds of thousands of American
farm families would be destroyed.

The feeling that man should live by providing goods
for his neighbors, not by withholding goods, goes very
deep; and I believe that it is spreading. But the condition
of greater balance and justice we now seek, in a capitalistic
structure hastily mended, can certainly not be obtained
by arranging that everybody work under the profit system
except the farmer. The farmer's instinct has always been
to be decent and unbusinesslike, to provide to the utter-
most, never to deny. This instinct, obeyed by millions of
scattered individuals in a society seeking profits and setting prices on a scarcity basis, took our farmers up the long
hill to the poorhouse; and killed them as customers. Their
death as consumers closed thousands of factories and
helped to throw millions out of work. Now we are trying
to give our farmers their rightful place in a more decent
and balanced system, a system that will work democratically and make for neighborliness and a shared abundance.
The people who raise the cry about the last hungry Chinamen are not really criticising the farmers or the AAA, but
the profit system, as we have inherited it from our past.

CHAPTER
XIII

TWELVE LONG YEARS

THE first exploring expedition to the new world was manned by farmers steeped in pioneer democracy whose minds and feelings had been deeply stirred when certain of their prices fell in 1921 to one-fifth of what they had been in 1920. One of the first boats they constructed for the purpose of reaching the land of social justice was christened "McNary-Haugen."

It was an ingenious craft of strange appearance, which was sunk in 1928 under the plea that it was a pirate ship. Nevertheless, the experience gained in building and launching this ill-fated vessel proved to be exceedingly useful when the day finally dawned that farmers seeking justice were not looked on in high quarters as merely pirates.

The farmers who started building boats at the time of the price smash in 1921 were of many kinds. Some were interested in an ark which would keep them afloat until the flood subsided; others wanted to float back into dreams of the good old days gone by. Older farmers who had lived during the farm agitations of the '80's and '90's were anxious to get aboard any sort of a boat because they knew that real trouble was ahead. They had seen what falling prices and burdensome farm mortgages had done during and after the Civil War, and some of them knew that the havoc after the Great War would be far greater.

Events soon justified their fears. The end of the World War had left the American farmer high and dry. Along with everybody else, but ten years ahead of most of them, he was perched on the stilts of high prices, high labor costs, high land values, and high debts. While Europe sowed its fields with high explosives, America was sowing more wheat to feed the men who made and fired the explosives, and did the actual killing. Acreage was expanded, new lands were bought for production, new machines hustled into use to take the place of high-priced labor.

When this wartime demand ceased, prices fell with a sick thud. But farm labor and machine costs slid down slowly, farm land values more slowly yet, and farm debts —including taxes—leaped. Wheat at two dollars pays two dollars' worth of taxes. Wheat at a dollar pays only a dollar's worth of taxes—but the tax bill still reads two dollars. Result: it takes twice as much wheat to pay the same taxes.

Agriculture cannot shut down as the shoe manufacturer can. In times of falling prices farm products pile up, and unfortunately they stay piled up for perhaps two or three years, but the surplus and the low prices fail to reduce production, because too many farmers have to increase production of dollar wheat in order to pay two-dollar mortgages and taxes. Freight rates, middleman's margins, debts, and taxes come down very slowly. They are among the prices that stay high. So also, many other industrial prices—prices the farmer pays for his machinery, his clothing, whatever he buys for living or for production—fail to drop as fast or as far as farm prices do. Some farmers lose their farms; nearly all lower their living standards and their standards of efficient production as a dwindling income prevents the use of fertilizer, essential hired labor, and soil-building practices, as the uneven deflation proceeds.

All this only repeats what usually happens after a Great War. It was more severe than usual in 1921 because the wartime prices were so high, because the consequent post-war deflation was accompanied by the loss of our foreign markets and the change in our status from a debtor to a creditor nation.

Those who recalled the agitations of the '80's and '90's were right in fearing a long period of painful readjustment after the World War. To them, the severity of the depression of 1921 was the call to arms. It was inevitable that many of the older men would look back to the grievances of the past.

Some of them had been connected with the Farmers' Alliance movement and were familiar with the doctrines of populism, free silver and greenbacks. They sensed that sooner or later there would be a money movement. One of the most radical and aggressive of these was John Simpson, who until his recent death was president of the Farmers' Union. Graduated from the University of Kansas in the '90's, he had written a thesis dealing with the economic causes and effects of war. He sold out his farm interests while prices were high early in 1920 and devoted his talents to organizing farmers to demand higher prices for their products, favoring free and unlimited coinage of silver at a ratio of 16 to 1 as one of the best ways of obtaining higher prices. The money issue, however, failed to excite much interest in 1921, or, in fact, until we were well into the 1930's.

The first significant post-war agricultural conference was the one called in January of 1922 by President Harding at the suggestion of my father, Henry C. Wallace, then Secretary of Agriculture. My father hoped that out of this conference might come a specific program of farm relief. Most of the Republican leadership, yearning for normalcy, seemed content to let normalcy be a synonym for inaction. The depression did spur Congress into exhaustive hearings on the state of agriculture, and to passage of the Packers and Stockyards Act, the Agricultural Credit Act, and the Capper-Volstead Act authorizing associations of agricultural producers, but none of these really got down to the root of the problem.

As I look back on that conference, I realize that it was conducted by men who were strongly imbued with the old pioneer spirit. They were rugged individualists, and proud of it. In the main, they had a right to be. Yet here they were appealing for collective, rather than individual, action. They found themselves up against a situation unlike any the pioneers, with their self-sufficient economy, had ever faced. They saw business and industry, though boasting of individualism, profiting by shrewd use of a delegated governmental power—federal subsidies in the form of tariffs, State and local franchises of one sort or another—largely at the expense of the rest of the population. In such a situation, what could one man on one farm do to protect his rights?

The old-time correctives did not meet the situation. Bimetallism, trust-busting, railroad-baiting, were beside the point. The George Peeks, the Frank Murphys, the Bill Hirths, the John Simpsons wanted to do something about agriculture itself. They wanted—quite unwittingly—to modify the farmer's rugged individualism for his own good. They didn't think of it that way, of course; but that is what any move to utilize the centralizing power of government amounts to. It was a new use for the pioneer spirit, and it could appeal only to those whose feeling of social injustice was strong enough to dominate their traditional individualism.

Out of this 1922 conference came 37 legislative recommendations; but there was not, as my father had hoped, any very definite and fundamental program of farm relief. One of the recommendations, however, looked a long way ahead, for it directed Congress and the President to "take steps immediately to reestablish a fair exchange value for all farm products with that of other commodities." Eleven years passed before a President and a Congress came along, in 1933, to take such steps by the passage of the Agricultural Adjustment Act.

The idea of fair exchange value had been described in a pamphlet published under the title, "Equality for Agriculture," and the authorship was unknown—until a second edition appeared addressed to J. R. Howard, then president of the American Farm Bureau Federation. On this edition the names of the authors appeared—George N. Peek and Hugh S. Johnson. Eleven years later George Peek, as Administrator of the AAA, was to help launch the first attempt to obtain fair exchange value for farmers, while his associate of 1922, General Johnson, was directing another great recovery effort, the NRA.

At the time Peek and Johnson were pamphleteering for equality for agriculture, both were connected with the Moline Plow Company. George Peek has frequently said that what impressed him with the need for farm relief was the fact that you couldn't sell a plow to a busted customer. He was influenced by more than that, of course, for he was farm-reared and thoroughly agrarian in his sympathies. I have known few men so determined and so little deterred by setbacks as George Peek in his long battle for the farmer.

He was his customary battling self at the 1922 conference. The idea of fair exchange value was finally approved, even if all of the Peek-Johnson plan was not. And their ratio plan of equality for agriculture so impressed the Secretary of Agriculture that he called together a small group of highly influential persons to consider it. Packers, millers, and New York financiers were present, among them Julius Barnes, Otto Kahn, Rufus Dawes, Thomas Wilson of Wilson & Company, Fred Wells of Minneapolis, and J. R. Howard and Gray Silver of the Farm Bureau.

The plan did not stir enthusiasm among this group, but it did give them food for thought. Most of them contented themselves with picking flaws. Otto Kahn, more kindly disposed, urged waiting six months or so to see if farm prices would not improve. Julius Barnes was extremely annoyed at the whole business, and even disapproved of calling the conference. Whether Mr. Barnes was at that time closely associated with the then Secretary of Commerce, Herbert Hoover, I do not know, but his

influence on the agricultural policy of Republican administrations seems to have been considerable. Secretary
Hoover, of course, was bitterly opposed to anything like
the Peek-Johnson ratio plan, as he was later opposed to
the McNary-Haugen plan. His later writings* indicated
that he favored the expansion of industrial exports but the
contraction of farm exports, without, however, providing
any mechanism for cushioning the shock of that contraction.

In the fall of 1923, Henry C. Wallace decided that something like the Peek-Johnson ratio plan was necessary, even
though the Administration of which he was a part was
antagonistic. The passage of the Fordney-McCumber Tariff Act, presumed to help the farmer, was a ghastly fraud
in the minds of economists generally and producers of
export crops specifically. With farm foreclosures on the
increase, with alarming bank failures in rural regions, and
with farm land values sinking fast, there was sufficient
impetus for the creation of a farm bloc in the Senate. This
group, looking with kindly eye on some farm measures,
attacked and killed a cooperative marketing bill which put
a measure of control over cooperatives in the Department
of Commerce. It was also instrumental in defeating Mr.
Mellon's first tax bill. The battle of the farm bloc with
Herbert Hoover was now under way.

At my father's suggestion the first McNary-Haugen bill
was drawn up by Charles J. Brand, then in the Department of Agriculture, later to become secretary of the
National Fertilizer Association. The essence of the

* See, for example, *The Country Gentleman* for January 10, 1925, and
the *Pacific Rural Press* for February 7, 1925.

McNary-Haugen idea was that farmers were to be given the centralizing power of the Federal Government so they could dump enough of their surplus abroad to raise prices in the domestic market. The loss on the stuff dumped abroad was to be paid by the farmers themselves by means of an equalization fee. In some versions, the price was to be raised so that producers of export crops could enjoy the full benefit of the tariff. In other versions the criterion was a price to be raised until it was as high relative to prices of things purchased by farmers as prevailed during 1909-14. This was the Peek-Johnson idea of fair exchange value. The feeling was in those days that there was an inexhaustible and complacent foreign market on which goods could be dumped at a low price without fear of retaliation.

The decision to proceed with this kind of legislation was not solely the product of any Washington conference, nor in response to the pressure of a few strong individuals. They merely reflected and concentrated a sentiment that existed very strongly in the West, as my father learned after he had sent Dr. H. C. Taylor, chief of the Bureau of Agricultural Economics, out west to study the situation first-hand,* and as Calvin Coolidge (who came to the Presidency in September, 1923) learned from reports of his special investigators, Frank Mondell and Eugene

* Doctor Taylor had not been out west very long, I am told, before Secretary Hoover began to sense danger in the mission. Hoover remonstrated with Harding, Harding remonstrated with my father, and my father conveyed the President's remonstrances to W. A. Shoenfeld, serving as acting chief of the Bureau of Agricultural Economics in Taylor's absence. When Shoenfeld wired Taylor that his presence was urgently needed in Washington, Taylor replied, "I left you in charge of the Bureau. Why don't you run it?" Taylor finished his trip.

Meyer. And when a State convention of North Dakota bankers approved the Peek plan and sent a delegation to Washington to endorse it, my father tentatively approved it, whereas Eugene Meyer firmly opposed it.

The first strong political support for the McNary-Haugen bill came, naturally enough, from Montana, Oregon, and other Northwestern wheat States. Congressman (now Senator) Dickinson of Iowa, who at that time was called by his conservative Republican colleagues "The Hell-raiser for Agriculture," came out to Iowa late in 1923 to preach McNary-Haugenism to the Iowa Farm Bureau Federation.

In the early days of the McNary-Haugen fight the cotton and tobacco people were decidedly lukewarm, although they saw in it interesting possibilities of embarrassing the conservative Republicans. The dairy people of the North and East were in many cases rather antagonistic, partly because of their conservative Republican background and partly because they honestly felt that the McNary-Haugen bill in action would increase their feed costs without increasing their incomes. Later the dairy leaders realized that the low prices for wheat, corn, and hogs were causing Western farmers to shift from these export crops into dairying. Milk, however, was not one of the eight basic commodities involved in the bill; the eight were wheat, corn, cotton, wool, cattle, sheep, swine, and rice.

The first McNary-Haugen bill, introduced in January, 1924, was defeated in the House on June 3 by a vote of 223 to 153. But the McNary-Haugenites had just begun to fight.

In July they organized the American Council of Agri-

culture after a meeting in St. Paul, and elected George
Peek president. Some highly practical political suggestions
were made at that meeting, and the groundwork was laid
for a future alliance between the farmers of the North and
the farmers of the South. That fall, just before he died,
my father brought Chester C. Davis from Montana for the
special purpose of working on the technique of the
McNary-Haugen Bill. Davis had attracted attention by his
intelligent work as Commissioner of Agriculture in Montana and as editor of *The Montana Farmer*. After the
death of Secretary Wallace, Chester Davis joined forces
with George Peek, who began his relentless four-year
drive for the passage of the McNary-Haugen Bill. During
the early years of the Coolidge Administration, he did not
have much success, but during the last two years, he was
able sufficiently to concentrate the opinion of warring
farm groups so that Congress twice passed the McNary-
Haugen Bill.

To fully half the population of the United States the
continued agitation for farm relief legislation in the years
1924 to 1929 doubtless seemed wholly unnecessary. How
silly to talk of farm relief when Radio Common was on
its way up to 500, when two cars for every garage were
just around the corner, when as a Nation we could boast
more miles of hard road and telephone line, more advertising, and more savings bank depositors than any two or
three others combined!

The fat years were here; there were not to be any more
lean ones, ever. Many important people said so. People
who wanted farm relief legislation were radicals and
crack-pots.

It was a false prosperity. It concealed the fact that farmers were losing their farms by hundreds of thousands. Between 1920 and 1933, one farm in every four was sold for debts or taxes. The New Era glorified high prices but ignored higher and older debts. It blithely rejoiced in foreign loans to support our foreign trade, and made repayment of the loans next to impossible by ever higher tariffs. It made of bigness in business and industry the crowning American virtue. Of the consequences of concentrated economic power it said nothing. Speculation was king; mass purchasing power was merely something to think about tomorrow. There was no time for farm relief.

The McNary-Haugen leaders did not see things that way. They knew what was happening out at the grass-roots. They knew that farm prices, though in better relationship to industrial prices than in 1921, were still too low. High land values, high debts, high taxes and a host of rigid production and living costs remained to plague the farmer. It would have required farm prices fully equal to industrial prices to remove that burden.

But it was not only the hang-over of wartime that oppressed agriculture; there were deep-lying forces in operation throughout the twenties, forces which moved independent of war. The scientist and the engineer were requiring adjustments of the farmer such as he had never faced before. The sweep of the wheat belt and the cotton belt to the West and the North meant new burdens of adjustment for those in the older parts of the regions. The migration of farm labor to the city invited the conquest of the prairie by the gas engine, and forced horses and mules out of use. That factor alone released 30 millions of acres of land from feed production, and made possible an equivalent expansion in cash crop production. Science has made it possible for American agriculture since the war to increase production 25 per cent without any increase in acreage. There had never been anything like that before. Swift changes in the national diet compelled changes in farm operations; improvements in methods of marketing and distribution brought distant producers close to market, but at the expense of producers already close by. The agricultural map of the country was constantly being redrawn.

In the long run forces of this sort are probably a gain, if a man can survive the first impact. Given some mechanism for collective action, farmers have a chance to make necessary adjustments swiftly and painlessly. Individually, they are helpless. McNary-Haugenism recognized as much, but the standpat national administration then at Washington did not. From Washington came only vetoes—and advice. Neither of these commodities paid the interest on the mortgage, nor the bill at the hardware store.

Considering the cities' preoccupation with their own prosperity, it is surprising that the McNary-Haugenites got as far as they did. By one means or another the Coolidge and Hoover Administrations did everything in their power to block them. The favorite method was to drag red herrings across the trail, to throw support to legislation less radical. The Agricultural Marketing Act of 1929, creating the Federal Farm Board, was the last of the herrings.

Back in the winter of 1924-25, with McNary-Haugenism rife, President Coolidge felt committed to calling into session a national agricultural committee. He chose the personnel very carefully, however, for he wanted no more official endorsements of the McNary-Haugen plan. He was successful. The committee met under the chairmanship of Robert D. Carey, now Senator from Wyoming, solemnly agreed on the need for higher protective tariffs on farm products, and approved the contraction of agriculture to domestic self-sufficiency "with only such foreign markets as shall be profitable." A bill supposed to attain these objectives was introduced, but it was defeated by the "co-op" group in the House, who again saw Hoover's hand at work.

The idea of having the cooperatives handle the surplus, with Federal aid, was winning support. The Dickinson bill, for instance, proposed this, and aroused the interest of the cotton cooperatives especially. It was apparent that some such concession would be necessary to swing the South to support of a McNary-Haugen bill.

Accordingly in March of 1926 farm leaders of the West and the South met in Memphis to see what common program could be developed. A Midwest Executive Committee of 22 had already been created in Des Moines in January, at the call of Governor Hammill of Iowa, and George Peek had been made chairman. The Memphis meeting paved the way for another session at Washington. It was then that amendments suitable to the South, and patterned after the Dickinson bill, were tacked onto the McNary-Haugen bill. In the next vote on the bill in the House, Southern votes for the first time, joined Western votes in support.

But every time the McNary-Haugenites made a gain,

the Administration pulled a new rabbit out of its hat. One time it would be a relatively innocuous concession to the cooperatives, such as the establishment of a Division of Cooperative Marketing in the Department of Agriculture. Another time it would be an increase in the tariff on wheat, or butter. Another time it might be a widely heralded move to finance the storage of surplus cotton, with Eugene Meyer as chairman. Nevertheless, the Administration was slowly but surely forced into much greater concessions than it wished to make. The apprehension was dawning that you couldn't beat something with nothing. Sooner or later a device that at least appeared to be substantial had to be pulled out of the hat, if McNary-Haugenism was not to triumph.

Such was the genesis of the Farm Board. There was the Fess bill, in 1926, giving a cooperative marketing division a fund of $100,000,000 with which to handle the surplus. There was the Curtis-Crisp bill of 1927, giving a Federal Farm Board a revolving fund of $250,000,000 with which to buy and withhold surpluses. Both of these had Administration approval, but they were defeated.

The climax of the McNary-Haugen fight came in 1928, when a much revised version passed both Houses of Congress, only to meet, for the second time, a Coolidge veto. The Senate voted to override the veto, but action in the House was blocked.

I have said that the 1928 veto was probably the climax in the long fight for McNary-Haugenism. The anti-climax came in the presidential campaign of the year. McNary-Haugenism began to fade out while other plans—export debenture, domestic allotment, stabilization—edged into the limelight.

In the 1928 presidential campaign, the McNary-Haugen bill and its equalization fee was a storm center first at the Republican Convention in Kansas City when Governor Lowden went down championing the farm cause, and again in the fall campaign, when Al Smith came out in favor of the equalization fee. As Secretary of Commerce, Herbert Hoover had been a steady opponent of the McNary-Haugen bill. George Peek, Chester Davis and others who had fought for the bill for four years recognized that the triumph of Hoover in 1928 meant an end, or at least a halt, to their hopes. It would be useless to fight for that principle as long as Hoover was President.

In the fall of 1928, he promised to help the farmer by means of higher tariffs and a Farm Board. Most farm leaders felt this was a political compromise to avoid doing something more fundamental—and radical—for agriculture. It was directly in line with the legislation introduced repeatedly to turn Congress away from McNary-Haugenism. It was also more or less representative of Hoover's views on farm relief as expressed while he was Secretary of Commerce. The rather broad powers given the Farm Board in the Agricultural Marketing Act of 1929 looked well on paper, but the hope persisted among Republican leaders that few of these powers would have to be used. The reluctance with which the Farm Board embarked on its stabilization operations is evidence of that.

Despite the political origin of the Farm Board, most farm leaders decided to give the Administration an opportunity to carry out this plan. The farm leaders' willingness in this matter was not reduced when it became noised about that the grain trade was not, after all, to run the show. The appointment of Alexander Legge as chairman painfully disappointed grain trade interests. Farmers who felt a traditional distrust of the International Harvester Corporation, of which Legge had been president, were perhaps skeptical of the appointment, but Legge's vigorous personality and his genuine affection for farming people seemed to put a better face on things.

Unfortunately for President Hoover, the Canadian wheat pool had for several years been trying to maintain world wheat prices by withholding wheat from the market. The Farm Board experiment in sustaining wheat prices was started at the worst possible moment, although no one fully realized it at the time. Chairman Legge of the Farm Board soon became convinced of the futility of trying to hold up wheat prices when there was no check on production. His picturesque language to wheat and cotton farmers illuminated the nature of the problem but did not help the immediate situation.

Shortly before this W. J. Spillman, a brilliant economist in the Department of Agriculture, had published a book called, *Balancing Agricultural Output*. Several men took up Spillman's idea, notably John D. Black, professor of agricultural economics at Minnesota and then at Harvard; Beardsley Ruml, professor of sociology at the University of Chicago; and M. L. Wilson, professor of agricultural economics at the Montana State Agricultural College. M. L. Wilson is now Assistant Secretary of Agriculture.

Dr. Black, who succeeded Joseph Davis as chief economist for the Farm Board, became more and more familiar with the Board's dilemma. He put some of his brightest young men to work on the details of a practical plan which would make it possible to adjust the output of American agriculture to the demand at a fair price. Among these young men the one who had the most faith in the Spillman idea was Mordecai Ezekiel.

Beginning in the fall of 1931, M. L. Wilson of Montana became a propagandist for the idea of the domestic allotment plan. He knew that the support of business men as well as farmers would be necessary. He wanted to familiarize all classes of society with the idea so that the plan could be put over in the next Administration.

By 1931 it had become apparent to the more intelligent supporters of the McNary-Haugen bill that export dumping would not work, not with European importing nations desperately trying to protect their own farmers' prices. The domestic allotment plan avoided that difficulty. It did not interfere with the open market price. It involved no attempt to keep the domestic price out of line with the world price, but rather rewarded producers who adjusted their production, by means of allotment payments which were in addition to the open market price. Since these benefit payments were only for that share of each grower's production which could be considered as for domestic consumption for human food, the scheme furnished a mechanism to prevent piling up a surplus for export at ruinous prices.

While the plan obviously might work better with some products than with others, it promised to be the most effective method available to improve the income of growers of staple crops, at least so long as the nation decided it wanted to remain on as highly protective a basis as it had since 1897. If the country finally began to weary of import duties, export bounties, and allotment rights, and showed a disposition to revise its trading policies, then the revision might be made all along the line.

Wilson did a good job of interesting many important leaders and groups in the domestic allotment plan. Governor Roosevelt, as Democratic candidate for President in 1932, became genuinely interested in the idea of controlling American farm production to fit the demand. The stabilization activities of the Farm Board, carried on without any means of controlling production other than by exhortation, convinced him of the need for a mechanism capable of action. Wilson's presentation of the allotment plan was brought to him by Rex Tugwell, and in a campaign speech at Topeka, Kansas, in September, the Democratic candidate described the essentials of what later became the Agricultural Adjustment Act.

After election, the President-elect asked several of us to meet with Marvin Jones, chairman of the House Agricultural Committee, in January of 1933 to see what could be done toward passing a bill of this sort in the 72nd Congress. This effort was unsuccessful. The opportunity did not finally come until the new Administration came into power in March of 1933.

I wish some skilled biographer might some day sketch the personalities involved in the long drawn-out campaign for farm relief from January of 1922 to the present moment. Some of these men have been colorful and powerful, others have been disinterested and long-suffering, still others have been bitter, mean and narrow, and a few have prostituted their talents, allowing selfish interests to throw confusion into the farm ranks. I have attended dozens of their meetings in Des Moines, St. Paul, Kansas City, Chicago and Washington. I have sat on their committees again and again while they have endeavored to frame a fresh bill of rights.

I think of Bill Hirth of Missouri, who has probably drawn more ringing resolutions than anyone else in the corn belt. I think of farm leaders who gave vent to their feelings in a magnificent manner regardless of monetary consequences. I think of Ed O'Neal who worked so unceasingly to heal the ancient breach between the Democratic farmers of the South and the Republican farmers of the Middle West. I think of other farm leaders who think chiefly in about the terms of the narrow group they represent, and strive to raise such issues as will enable them to hold on to their salaries as long as possible.

There are still others who have grown wise in the ways of men and who at the same time retain a sincere desire of benefiting not only farmers but all humanity. These last speak cautiously but on occasion fearlessly. They are the salt of the earth, and they will be heard in the development of any comprehensive national policy.

Many people speak slightingly of the farm leaders, but it is my observation that they compare very favorably with the leaders of labor, of industry and of finance. While some of them have a narrow nationalistic class outlook, there are just as many men of truly broad statesmanship as among the leaders of the other groups. Their internal jealousies are no greater; their patriotic statesmanship is fully as high.

The farm group, in my opinion, has been more definitely responsible for preparing the way for present changes in this country than any other section of our population. Long before any other group they were forced to consider the fundamentals of national prosperity under post-war conditions. Their distress came first. Their land frontier had disappeared. Their suffering so sharpened their insight that they became capable of thinking in terms of balanced relationship between the producing and consuming forces. The nature of their calling was such that they caught the point of view of both business and labor.

Their efforts to invent and build a modern vessel with which to reach a new world, their experiences and failures should be of value now to business and labor. Because such a high percentage of their export crops find a market overseas, farmers are forced to think more definitely in world terms than any other large section of our population. This situation for a time played havoc with their psychology, because instinctively they disliked foreigners. Psychological suffering, however, often produces the best pioneers.

CHAPTER
XIV

THE THIRTEENTH YEAR

In THE thirteenth year, 1933, the farm organizations, with the help of the Department of Agriculture, built a boat which Congress and the President approved as seaworthy. The design complied in the main with the specifications set forth by Governor Roosevelt in his Topeka speech of September, 1932. The craft was launched May 12, 1933, and immediately set on a course toward social justice. At this writing we have not reached our destination, but our farming people are proceeding with confidence, and they have made remarkable progress, on the whole. They believe Congress and the President will give them a new boat or renovate the old one, if the Agricultural Adjustment Act of May 12, 1933, does not prove sufficiently powerful and flexible.

Most level-headed people who know the facts will agree that during 1933 and 1934 the farm expedition proceeded as rapidly as was safe and practical. The voyage starting on March 8, 1933, has been an exciting one, through many storms. I propose here to tell something of the mechanics of building the boat and some of the storms we have managed to weather.

When the call for a special session of the new Congress was sent out on March 5, the general idea in Administration circles was that Congress was to remain in session three days only, to meet the banking emergency. Rex Tugwell and I thought, however, that it might be possible to pass agricultural legislation at this exceedingly short session. We took the matter up with President Roosevelt the evening of March 8, and immediately thereafter got in touch over long-distance telephone with farm leaders we could reach late that night. We called them to Washington for March 10, to see if they could agree on farm legislation.

Despite the short notice, about 50 farm organization and farm paper representatives appeared. Because of the banking emergency some of them had trouble getting cash to pay railroad fare, but somehow they got to Washington.

They came prepared, I believe, to agree to any reasonable proposal. The new atmosphere in Washington, the drama of the inauguration and the bold action taken in dealing with the banking crisis, had its effect. The form of the emergency banking legislation particularly with its transfer of broad powers by Congress to the Executive, impressed them. Three of the farm representatives went so far as to draft a tentative proposal by which Congress might transfer to the President, and through him to the Secretary of Agriculture equally broad powers for dealing with the farm crisis.

The conference lasted a day and a half. There were no long speeches. There was no rehashing of familiar facts. There was solid agreement on the necessity for action. The proposal to grant broad authority to the Executive fell on receptive ears; but there were also words of caution. The question as to what plan could best be applied to cotton, what to wheat, to dairy products, and so on, aroused the most discussion.

Once or twice, it looked as if this might be the rock the conference would split on. Men from the cotton, wheat, and corn areas were strong for some plan of leasing acres out of production, the wheat men particularly showing a preference for the domestic allotment idea. The cattle men were less certain. Representatives of the dairy cooperatives were perhaps most skeptical of all. Nevertheless, they agreed to go along, provided they were left free to approve or reject any plan which might directly involve their industry. The upshot of the discussion was the proposal to make the legislation so flexible that the Secretary could apply whatever scheme seemed best adapted to a given commodity.

The idea of parity, of fair exchange value for farm products, which George Peek and Hugh Johnson brought to the 1922 farm conference, was agreed upon as the objective of the new legislation. Parity, it was thought, serves not only as a goal to shoot at, but as a limiting factor in deference to consumers. It was believed that all fair-minded consumers would see the justice in getting purchasing power of farm products back to a satisfactory level, but that they would want some device to prevent farm prices from going unfairly high. The years 1909-14, chosen as the base period from which parity is figured, had long been considered by farm economists as the period with the most satisfactory relationships between the farm group and other major producing groups.

Saturday noon after a conference with the President, we were given the word to draft a bill and proceed full-steam ahead. That was March 11. On March 16 the bill was introduced in the House by Marvin Jones, chairman of the House Committee on Agriculture, to the accompaniment of that famous message from the President in which he offered the bill as frankly an experiment on "an untrod path."

Between the decision on March 11 and the introduction of the bill on March 16, a great deal had to be done. To make provision for flexibility in the bill; to give the Secretary of Agriculture power to make contracts to reduce acreage with millions of individuals, and power to make marketing agreements with processors and distributors; to transfer to the Secretary, even if temporarily, the power to levy processing taxes; to express in legislation the concept of parity—all these points, and a thousand others, were unorthodox and difficult to express even by men skilled in the law.

There have been many weird stories as to the authorship of the Adjustment Bill. Some said Mordecai Ezekiel, economic advisor to the Secretary, wrote the bill. Some said it was all a Red plot of Rex Tugwell's. Occasionally I was suspected of having had something to do with it.

As a matter of fact a great many people contributed to the drafting of the bill. The legal job was done chiefly by Fred Lee, for many years legislative counsel for the Senate, and by Jerome Frank, who later became general counsel for the Adjustment Administration. Ezekiel, Tugwell, and myself, from the Department, and George Peek, Chester Davis, and Charles Brand, among others, saw to it that the bill carried out the wishes of the farm leaders' conference. Several Congressional leaders contributed important suggestions. Though the bill was written under pressure of time, and at the cost of a good deal of sleep, the bill was in many respects a logical crystallization of the long struggle for adequate farm legislation, and it endeavored to avoid the weaknesses and obstacles which had wrecked all earlier proposals.

To those in Congress and outside who were familiar with the farm problem and farm relief legislation, the bill seemed simply the fulfillment of the promise the President made in a campaign speech at Topeka the preceding autumn. To a good many city dailies, however, and to many Congressmen, I fear, the farm bill seemed a fearful and wonderful thing. The idea of conceiving a bill as a piece of social machinery—as something to help restore balance between major producing groups—did not register with the natural opponents of such an idea. To a majority of farmers, however, judging by the reports that came to us, the bill did offer the first ray of hope in many a long year. It began to appear that the new Administration meant business. I recall how strong that feeling was after the Roosevelt landslide, and how one farmer walked into my office in Des Moines, shortly after election in 1932, and said, "I was going to tell the loan company to take my farm, but now I'm going to make a fight to hold it. It looks to me, for the first time in years, as if we farmers had a chance."

Some hoped that the bill would become law within two

or three weeks, but that was too much to expect. Congress did well to dispose of it in two months. The idea of flexibility in legislation was new, and had to be explained and justified. The concept of fair exchange value, like any problem of economic relationships, was too abstract for a good many minds to grasp. The allotment scheme, which really is complex, was a stumbling-block even for friends of the measure. And, of course, the proposal to transfer broad powers to the Executive, even though subject to recall at the will of Congress, seemed risky to many firm believers in Jeffersonian democracy.

For a time some of the processing and distributing trades, through their lobbies, threatened effective opposition. They were fearful of the processing tax, but their fears were somewhat moderated by the hope of marketing agreements, obtainable under the bill, which would permit them some freedom from the restrictions of the anti-trust laws.

There was never much doubt that the bill would pass, but there were moments when the noise of contending groups grew pretty loud. A good many of them descended on me, and I was glad to get their points of view, even if they frequently left behind more heat than light.

At one extreme were the left-wing farmers, whose grievance could not be gainsaid, demanding $1.50 wheat and $10 hogs inside of six weeks. At the other extreme were the more hard-boiled among the middlemen, who insisted on the right to run their businesses as they pleased regardless of the consequences. Each group seemed so sure it was right that I knew it never would be possible to expect much cooperation from them. Consequently, when the job of administering the law did come along, I knew we would be living in a veritable hell, and I thought it best to say as much before Congressional committees and other groups. I didn't want anybody harboring any illusions about the new machinery.

The most notable difference of opinion in the Congressional debate developed around the so-called "cost of production" amendment. John Simpson, president of the Farmers' Union, was unable to attend the first farm meeting and was very anxious to have included in the bill a scheme for fixing prices, by means of compulsory control of marketing, at a point equal to cost of production. I felt there was grave danger in fixing prices without the control of production and I knew that until payrolls in the cities were very decidedly increased, it would not be possible to fix the prices of farm products at a point high enough to represent the Farmers' Union idea of cost of production without backing up on the farm a very considerable portion of the food which normally goes to the city. I therefore requested the Congressional conference committee to strike out the cost of production amendment. Something of this sort may eventually be necessary. The whole idea is so complex that it is discussed separately in Chapter X.

While Congress debated, cotton was sprouting on an expanded acreage. Winter wheat was ripening. Spring wheat was going in. Hog and cattle numbers were reaching record levels, and the dairy industry was wrestling with more than its annual spring surplus. Enactment of the farm bill on May 12 left little time for effective action on 1933 crops.

The new machinery, crude and untried, awaited expert assemblers and operators. It could be made to work, I felt, if enough people wanted it to work. But the first requirement was to select the men who would be most likely to assemble and operate it sympathetically and understandingly.

The obvious place to look for such men was among those who for so many years had fought for the right to build such machinery. Soon after the bill was introduced I had sounded out George Peek for the post of administrator, and, for other positions of importance, Charles J. Brand, who drafted the first McNary-Haugen bill, Chester Davis, first lieutenant to Peek in the farm fight, and M. L. Wilson, the successful evangelist of the domestic allotment plan.

Peek's business experience, his aggressiveness, and his unvarying sympathy for farmers, among other qualities, seemed to recommend him for the job of making the new machinery work. Accordingly I presented his name to the President. Shortly after the bill was signed, the appointment of Mr. Peek as administrator of the Agricultural Adjustment Administration was announced. Because of Mr. Brand's familiarity with many agricultural trades, and his encyclopedic knowledge of the processing and distributing as well as production of farm products, he was named co-administrator. It was expected that he would concern himself particularly with marketing agreements and codes. Chester Davis seemed the logical man to have charge of the other principal function, the adjustment of production by agreement with farmers. M. L. Wilson, with his intimate knowledge of the wheat problem as well as the domestic allotment plan, was an immediate choice for the head of the wheat section.

Necessarily, the ideas which some of these men fought for in the 1920's had to be modified to fit the world situation in the 1930's. George Peek and Charles Brand held rather strongly to their original McNary-Haugen conceptions of export sales at less than the domestic market, whereas Chester Davis, who had become especially familiar with M. L. Wilson's ideas, realized from the start the necessity of reducing acreage.

Even before these appointments had been made, and before the bill had become law, we found prospective co-operators under the Act sitting on our doorstep. Wheat growers, though dubious of any action on the 1933 crop, wanted to get plans under way for some action on the 1934 crop which would go into the ground in the fall of 1933. Cotton producers and textile operators alike, desperate at what 5-cent cotton had done to the South, were ready to do anything that promised fairly immediate relief. Representatives from milk cooperatives and milk distributors in Chicago, Cincinnati, and elsewhere, were anxious to shove marketing agreements through the mill in order to raise prices and profits to all concerned.

One moment we concentrated on new personnel for the AAA, the next moment we devoted to deciding just how the new machinery ought to fit together. The corridors of the Administration Building were crowded with farmers, farm leaders, processors, and reporters, each with dozens of insistent questions, few of which could be answered then and there. From early morn until midnight and often later, delegations of dairymen, cotton growers, wheat growers, cling peach producers from California, and many others filed in and out of our offices seeking the way to make the new machinery whir into action in their behalf. Those were hectic days. Somehow we got through them though it was a rare day when an irresistible desire didn't crash into an immovable fact, with heavy damage to frayed nerves.

As the machinery was set up, we were able to act simultaneously on several commodities. While our lawyers and milk experts were drawing up marketing agreements for some of the larger city milksheds, our wheat and cotton sections were preparing for action on those products, in each case, however, in consultation with the producers and processors involved. We were unwilling to proceed with any program unless we knew an overwhelming majority of the industry would approve it.

In mid-June we were able to announce a plan of action for wheat and cotton producers. Two or three weeks before we had called to Washington the representatives of about twenty-five wheat producing, processing, and consuming organizations for a public conference. We had no carefully prepared plan, but we knew that we had in that room all the elements necessary for one. Naturally, the domestic allotment plan was uppermost in the minds of most, for it had been the most talked of plan for two or three years previous.

Ordinarily, if you put a wheat farmer, a miller, a grain trader, a baker, and a consumer, in one room to agree on a plan to raise wheat prices, you would not be optimistic about the possibilities. On this occasion, however, the pressure of a farm crisis was behind them, compelling action. And many, I believe, had become convinced that you can't have an enduring national prosperity without farm prosperity. Strange to say it was the late Henry Stude, secretary of the bakers' organization, who made one of the most eloquent pleas for a wheat program.

The conferees did not agree on every point; far from it; but they did agree to go along on a plan, and the domestic allotment principle seemed to meet with the least opposition. The grain trade generally thought we should do everything possible to encourage exports; the millers were apprehensive about a processing tax on flour; nevertheless, they did not press their opposition as they might have been expected to do.

A wheat carryover three times the normal, no hope for exports, another crop coming on, and prices far below parity suggested drastic action. One proposal, therefore, was to rent sufficient wheat land out of the 1933 crop to keep the carryover down. That would have involved plowing under growing wheat.

Fortunately, this proposal was hardly advanced before the crop reports showed a sensational reduction in winter wheat prospects because of unfavorable weather. It would not be necessary to plow under growing wheat; nature had already done it—unequally, cruelly, to be sure, but decisively, and without provoking the resentment of consumers. Our press section breathed a sigh of relief; it would not be necessary to write about the logic of plowing under wheat while millions lacked bread. I say this, it should be understood, seriously, for our traditional economy is an economy of scarcity, and it so happens that the larger the piles of surplus wheat in Kansas, the longer are the breadlines in New York. Crazy, perhaps, but quite orthodox in a society which still plays the game according to the rules of scarcity.

The plan finally adopted was the domestic allotment plan for making payments to each wheat producer on the basis of his proportionate share of the national production that was domestically consumed. In return for that benefit payment, the producer would agree to reduce his wheat acreage in the 1934 and 1935 crops by such percentage, not to exceed 20 per cent, as the Secretary of Agriculture should determine. In other words, acreage reduction was to be made to pay the individual farmer. Past appeals to reduce acreage had always fallen on deaf ears because no man could be sure his neighbors would follow suit; in fact, some might think it shrewd to expand acreage instead. The new wheat plan permitted individual interest to coincide with group interest.

Because the reduction in the 1933 crop by nature had left thousands of growers with little or nothing to sell, it was decided to make the first payments—comprising about two-thirds of the total payment—as early that fall as possible, and to base them on at least three years' production. In July and August, therefore, the Adjustment Administration and the Agricultural Extension Service, State and Federal, began the considerable task of acquainting more than a million wheat growers with the details of the wheat adjustment program.

The situation in the Cotton Belt was more desperate,

for along with a carryover three times the normal and with a price less than half of fair exchange value, an increased cotton acreage and unusually favorable weather promised to keep prices low, or drive them even lower. Not only cotton farmers and farm leaders, but textile men and other business men from the South came up to Washington to insist that the South simply could not endure another winter of 5-cent cotton.

For one or two precious weeks, however, we were held back by the testimony of certain very experienced cotton traders who favored cheap cotton because it enabled them to sell in foreign markets in increased volume, with correspondingly increased commissions. When it became quite apparent that these gentlemen had little interest in the general plight, we were able to work out a plan for effective, if drastic, action.

That plan involved plowing under about 10 million acres—a fourth of the total—of growing cotton. Growers would receive benefit payments sufficient to make the plow-up feasible. The money to finance the program was to come from processing taxes, as in the wheat plan.

But would the majority of cotton farmers be willing to plow up standing cotton? We knew that instinctively they would dislike the idea of destroying a growing crop just as much as we did. But it was either that or 5-cent cotton.

Working at tremendous pressure, the Adjustment Administration prepared the necessary contracts, got out instruction sheets and explanatory leaflets, and set to work to sign up a million or more cotton growers in this campaign to plow under 10 million acres of cotton. The energy and spirit put into that drive by some 22,000 volunteer local leaders and extension agents, were truly extraordinary. The physical task of making individual contact with a million farmers is in itself considerable; when to that task is added the job of explaining a complicated contract (a form of option on government-owned cotton was also offered along with the benefit payment for the plow-up), and of driving home the economic situation the Cotton Belt was up against, it can be seen that we had some reason to fear that the program might not go over.

Yet within a few weeks the job was done, and in August a million farmers plowed under 10 million acres of cotton. Later in the year, they received over a hundred million dollars in benefit payments in return for the plow-up, and they had the satisfaction of seeing a potential 17-million-bale crop—which surely would have meant 5-cent cotton —kept down to 13 million bales. They also had the satisfaction of seeing the price of cotton double, both because of the plow-up and because of the President's monetary policy.

I confess I have always had mingled feelings about this plow-up campaign. It was an amazing demonstration of what a united people can do because they know there is no acceptable alternative. In company with the monetary policy and other measures, it did succeed, to be sure, in raising the farm value of the cotton crop from 464 million dollars in 1932 to 851 million dollars, including AAA payments, in 1933, with immediate results not only on the farm but in increased business in village and city not only down South but elsewhere. We have a trunkful of documentary evidence on that. Nevertheless, to have to destroy a growing crop is a shocking commentary on our civilization. I could tolerate it only as a cleaning up of the wreckage from the old days of unbalanced production. Certainly none of us ever want to go through a plow-up campaign again, no matter how successful a price-raising method it proved to be.

While the cotton and wheat campaigns were absorbing the interest of two great farming regions, the device for financing them was attracting more and more attention among consumers and, more particularly, among those who manufactured wheat and cotton into bread and cloth. For the protection of consumers, the Adjustment Act specified that the farmer's share of the consumers' dollar might not exceed the share he got in the base period, 1909-14. In addition, the Act authorized the Secretary of Agriculture, to make public his findings as to the effect of the processing tax on both producers and consumers, and permitted the weapon of publicity to prevent pyramiding of the tax. To accomplish these ends a consumers' division in the AAA was necessary. This was established, with Frederic C. Howe in charge.

Anticipating inflation and reduced production, wheat prices began to rise sensationally, and bread began to follow suit. Much of the rise in bread prices, however, was blamed on the imposition of the processing tax on flour, amounting to 30 cents a bushel in terms of wheat and about a half a cent a loaf in terms of bread. The fact that between 1929 and 1933 bread prices had not fallen in anywhere near the same proportion as wheat prices, seemed to be overlooked.

When prices were declining, of course, it was customary

for some of the baking interests to explain that the price of wheat was a negligible factor in the price of bread, and that labor and distribution charges—which stayed high— were chiefly responsible for relatively high bread prices. But in the spring and summer of 1933, with wheat prices responding to monetary and weather influences, the prevailing explanation for the higher bread prices was that wheat had gone up, and that the processing tax was a large factor. Later, increased labor costs under the NRA were also presented to explain the higher bread prices.

In July I pointed out that an increase in the retail price of a pound loaf from 6½ to 8 cents was probably justified, but that any greater increase was open to question. A good many bakers, of course, kept their prices fairly constant, but reduced the weight of the loaf.

The bakers' organization was quick to resent any charge of undue increases in prices. On several occasions exchange of comments between the bakers and the Consumers' Counsel became somewhat heated. Nevertheless, the result was that bread prices stayed fairly well in line, and the people of the country got a practical education in the true costs of a loaf of bread. Some leaders in the baking industry helpfully used their influence to keep less enlightened individual bakers from putting over unwarranted price increases.

Prices of cotton goods did not stay in line quite as well. At a press conference in my office I laid before the correspondents the evidence of what was happening. The price of raw cotton at that time—mid-July—was around 11 cents, but the textile industry was pricing cotton sheeting on the basis of 18-cent cotton, print cloth on the basis of 17.6-cent cotton. Between March 1 and the second week in July prices of print cloth had advanced 116 per cent, sheeting 118 per cent, and yarn 102 per cent. Raw cotton prices, meanwhile, had advanced only 77 per cent. The finished goods were selling at prices 30 per cent above their usual relation to raw cotton prices.

What had happened, as nearly as we could determine, was that the textile industry was anticipating the processing tax on raw cotton, scheduled to go into effect on August 1 at the rate of 4.2 cents a pound. Also, the industry was anticipating increased labor costs under their NRA code. Apparently enough of this sort of thing was done to absorb all of the increased costs, when they did come, without further increases to consumers.

Again, as with the bakers, the publicity given cotton cloth costs did not win the undying gratitude of the textile people, but it may have had some effect in public education. I cannot say that it had much effect in keeping down the prices of cotton goods. Perhaps that was too much to expect, because the immediate reason for higher prices was the rush of orders which descended on manufacturers. A higher price was therefore the normal competitive reaction to speculative buying by distributors. According to our studies, textile operators as a whole seem to have increased their margins as well as prices, and to have fattened their profits appreciably during much of 1933. Later, when increased prices reduced retail sales, they responded by declaring an "emergency" and reducing production for a time.

So far as the Adjustment Administration was concerned, it could only direct its attention to false claims about the effect of the processing tax on prices, and publicity was about the only weapon it could use. No amount of publicity, I suppose, could counteract the repeated but casual remarks of retailers on how overalls formerly selling at $1 a pair, because of the processing tax now cost $1.75. Actually, the processing tax could account for only 8 cents of the rise.

These mounting retail prices did not simplify our problem in the Midwest, where thus far only a wheat program had been announced, and where the corn-hog industry was staggering under impossibly low prices, excessive supplies, closed foreign markets and low domestic purchasing power. With so many of us in Washington coming from the Corn Belt, it seemed strange to the people out there that nothing had been done as yet to help solve their problems.

It was not from any lack of interest, but from an inability to see any way to help the Corn Belt, at least within a few months. When we contemplated some form of the domestic allotment plan applied to hogs, we shuddered at the complications. When we tried to figure out an acreage rental plan for corn, we came up against the intimate relationship between corn and hogs; we couldn't adjust either one, without being prepared at the same time to adjust the other. Conferences by the score began and ended in my office, and as often as not many of us were ready to give up the problem as too tough.

Plenty of pressure for action came from the country, but it was not accompanied by any helpful blueprints. Finally, it was decided that somehow the corn-hog growers must be induced to say precisely what they wanted, and what sort of program they would be willing to push. The wheat and cotton growers had done that, and it seemed wise to insist on the same local initiative from the Corn Belt.

The best we had been able to work out was a long-time program to reduce 1934 corn acreage by at least 10 million acres, and reduce hog numbers (by breeding fewer sows) by at least 7 million head. The two had to go together, to avoid future maladjustments. But the price effects of this program would not be felt until late in 1934, in all probability; how could corn-hog farmers continue to exist on $2.50 hogs and 35-cent corn?

We had no answer to the question, but before long producers themselves did. From committees of representative Corn Belt farmers came this suggestion: During September 1st the Government slaughter five or six million little pigs, and perhaps a couple of million piggy sows, in order to reduce the tonnage of pork to be marketed later in the winter. By slaughtering pigs at under 100 pounds, instead of at the normal weight of over 200 pounds, the pressure of supply on the market would be less in late winter and prices would then rise. The edible portions of the carcasses, it was agreed, could be distributed by the Federal Emergency Relief Administration to those on relief.

Those corn-hog farmers who looked ahead any distance knew that vast numbers of hogs were destined to come to market during the winter of 1933-34 because the cheap corn of the preceding year had stimulated a great expansion in breeding operations. They foresaw $2 hogs, and in many cases no market at all. They were willing to take a drastic step to avoid a disastrous future.

While we felt the scheme would boost hog prices by the following February, when the slaughtered little pigs would normally have gone to market at heavier weights, nevertheless we saw three grave dangers in the plan: First, the public reaction; second, the possibility of an unsatisfactory arrangement with the packers who did the slaughtering; and third, the fear that the Corn Belt would be unwilling to follow this short-time plan with a more fundamental plan involving corn acreage.

It was a foregone conclusion that the public would not like the idea of slaughtering baby pigs. Doubtless it is just as inhumane to kill a big hog as a little one, but few people would appreciate that. They contended that every little pig has the right to attain before slaughter the full pigginess of his pigness. To hear them talk, you would have thought that pigs are raised for pets. Nor would they realize that the slaughter of little pigs might make more tolerable the lives of a good many human beings dependent on hog prices. We simply had to make up our minds to face an unfavorable public reaction, despite the diversion of 100,000,000 pounds of baby pork to relief channels.

The problem of arranging for the slaughter of the hogs by the packers was likewise difficult, but by calling for competitive bids in the usual governmental fashion we hoped to keep costs within reason.

The most important consideration of all, to my mind, was the understanding that this program was superficial, and that it must be followed in 1934 by something much more fundamental. So in announcing the emergency slaughter program, in the course of an address August 18 at the Chicago fair, I said we were proceeding on the assumption that this program would be followed by a program in 1934 and perhaps 1935 involving both corn acreage and hog numbers. The slaughter program was to be financed later on by a processing tax on hog products, which could also finance the program to be adopted for 1934.

I was terribly concerned lest the Corn Belt fail to see how dangerous this drastic slaughter program could be, if not tied up to a reduction in corn acreage in 1934. The after-effects could be disastrous to hog prices in 1934-35. Not one farmer in a hundred, it seemed, realized what a terrible mess the Corn Belt would be in, unless it promptly dug deep both in thinking and action.

But if this was true of the corn-hog industry at that time, it was much more true of the dairy industry. While we were groping for some solution for excessive supplies of dairy products and low prices, the dairy industry was continuing to ignore the basic influence of supply and demand and was preferring to rely on ever higher tariff barriers both nationally, through the usual import duties on dairy products and fats and oils, and locally through the use of health regulations and other devices in limiting the supplies coming into the city milksheds. The intimate relationship between city prosperity and dairy income carried over, of course, into the depression, when low city incomes meant low dairy incomes. In addition, cattle numbers had reached the highest level in our history, and years of relatively high prices for fluid milk had lured more and more midwestern farmers into dairying, until the pressure of excess supplies at low prices was disrupting not only butter and cheese markets, but fluid milk markets as well.

Only a national production control program could really ease the dairy situation, it seemed to us, but how to go about securing such production control, and how to dissuade many of the dairy leaders from reliance on such false supports as higher tariffs and higher walls around milksheds, was not at all clear. At that stage, we only knew that some such program must eventually be devised, and that our experience with cotton, wheat, and tobacco was encouraging enough to warrant comparable action on other products. The fact that a million cotton growers had met their emergency problem head on, and that more than half a million wheat growers representing 77 per cent of the acreage were responding to the wheat plan, suggested that dairymen would respond equally well.

When butter prices began to slump under the pressure of huge stocks in the summer of 1933, the dairy leaders united in agreeing that it was time for the Government to help. They did not propose production control. They simply proposed that the Government buy up a large amount of butter and take it off the market, letting the future take care of itself.

This was so much like the Farm Board stabilization efforts that we recoiled from the idea. When prices kept on dropping, however, I said we might consider a butter purchase plan provided the dairy industry would devise and support a national production control plan later on. Both the butter purchases and the production control plan would have to be financed, of course, by a processing tax on dairy products.

There was no enthusiasm for production control, particularly since it involved a processing tax. Dairy leaders feared the effect of such a tax on consumption, and of course they were perfectly right in questioning that. Under the Adjustment Act, however, no other course was possible.

Finally, after a good deal of shifting for position, it was decided to have the Government buy up perhaps 60 million pounds of butter for distribution through relief channels, and to follow this plan with a production control program, both to be financed by a moderate processing tax. It was fairly certain that the butter purchases would give butter prices a chance to recover, and the industry's promise to go along on a production control plan later indicated that a temporary improvement might be converted into a fairly permanent one.

The paradox of want in the midst of plenty was constantly in our minds as we proceeded with schemes like the emergency hog slaughter and the butter purchase. To many of us, the only thing that made the hog slaughter acceptable was the realization that the meat and lard salvaged would go to the unemployed.

This feeling was so general in Administration circles that in October, 1933, there was organized the Federal Surplus Relief Corporation, with Harry Hopkins chairman, and with Secretary Ickes and myself serving with Hopkins on the governing board. At last we had a mechanism through which the surplus could reach the hungry. Of course the Federal Emergency Relief Administration was in part such a mechanism, but it could not utilize existing surpluses as directly and effectively as the new corporation could.

Not many people realized how radical it was,—this idea of having the Government buy from those who had too much, in order to give to those who had too little. So direct a method of resolving the paradox of want in the midst of plenty doubtless could never have got beyond the discussion stage before 1933. At the time I hoped the Corporation might be empowered to buy up industrial as well as agricultural surpluses, in so far as relief needs warranted, and some of this has been done. So far as the AAA was concerned, it could now proceed with its task of adjusting production to the needs of the American people, rather than merely to the buying power of the American people. It became possible to attack the surplus problem from both top and bottom, treating it as a result of both overproduction and under consumption, the degree of each varying widely, to be sure, with the commodity. The new Corporation could not absorb all of our farm surpluses, but it could give us new assurances that no one would go hungry or ragged because of any of our adjustment programs.

At the same time we were not forgetting the foreign market, even though our agricultural exports had shrunk drastically. The Administration as a whole was setting the stage for action on reciprocal tariffs, and the Agricultural Adjustment Administration was trying out two special devices to ease the pain of the wheat surplus. One device was an international wheat agreement; the other was an export subsidy mechanism for our surplus white wheat in the Pacific Northwest.

Our domestic allotment plan was keyed into the international wheat agreement developed, with the help of the State Department, at London in the summer of 1933. The agreement provided for a reduction in acreage and exports in the four great exporting nations (Argentina, Australia, Canada, and the United States), and an agreement on the part of the importing nations to go no further with their tariffs, quotas, and other trade-restricting measures. In line with that agreement our reduction in acreage for the 1934 crop was fixed at 15 per cent.

At the very outset the odds were against the success of a worldwide agreement, but to us that seemed no valid reason for not trying to develop one. There was everything to gain and nothing to lose. As I write, the fate of the agreement is uncertain; it may be that some of the exporting countries will find it impossible to develop a technic to control production; but I am convinced that sooner or later some such technic will have to be developed.

The other device, the export subsidy for our Pacific Northwest wheat, necessarily had to be utilized carefully in order to avoid conflict with the international agreement. Wheat and flour sold by the specially organized Pacific Wheat Export Corporation went to the Orient, but in order to avoid doing an injustice to Australia, it was necessary to time shipments to avoid depressing prices in the Orient.

Because of the disparity between the world price and the American price for wheat, these exports were subsidized at the rate of about 22 cents a bushel, the money for the subsidy coming from the processing tax on wheat. Even with this subsidy, it was difficult to place the wheat, especially after China had increased her tariff on wheat and flour. About 35 million bushels of Northwest wheat were disposed of in this way, but with increasing difficulty.

It is becoming more and more apparent that most of the world will not tolerate subsidized exports. I have long suspected this, but I was convinced of it last February when our subsidized exports of wheat to China were paralleled by Poland's attempts to land subsidized rye on our shores.

Six months after the Adjustment Act had become law, we could look back on a summer of unprecedented activity in assembling and operating a new piece of social machinery. The progress of ideas in a dozen years had finally reached the point of action: First the McNary-Haugenites wanted to dump the surplus abroad; deterred from doing that, farmers agreed, half-heartedly, to let the Farm Board try withholding it; when that failed, the hope of dumping surpluses abroad was also gone, and there was no alternative but the direct and logical plan of trying to prevent surpluses from coming into existence.

A plow-up campaign buried some of the cotton surplus; a wheat program and a tobacco program were promising to keep wheat and tobacco surpluses from mounting higher; the slaughter of 6 million little pigs made a small dent in the surplus of pork and lard; and a variety of marketing agreements were at work in city milksheds, and among producers and processors of tobacco and certain special crops to provide adequate prices and fair market practices.

Processing taxes had gone into effect on wheat, cotton, tobacco, and pork products, and the proceeds, in the form of benefit payments, were beginning to reach the grass roots. Premium on hogs for the emergency slaughter were augmenting the cash income of the Corn Belt and rescuing some farmers menaced by drought; butter purchases were stabilizing butter prices, 92-score butter being kept at 22 cents or above for several months. Monetary policy, acreage adjustment programs, and NRA codes boosting factory payrolls and employment were combining to improve the domestic market for farm products. Meanwhile, the burden of debt was in process of reduction, or at least alleviation, through the work of the Farm Credit Administration.

Necessarily we could not be sure how all our plans would work. Along an "untrod path" there is no telling what dangers and obstacles you will meet. But we were beginning to have the comfortable feeling that the new machinery was lumbering into effective action. Economic results could not yet be measured, but reports from the wheat States, especially, told of a genuine revival of the old New England town-meeting idea in the county production control associations. In making individual acreage allotments add up to a total that jibed with government statistics, farmers were doing a significant job of economic self-government. Though in this and all the other programs there was opportunity for disastrous friction, the human will to make the machinery function was more powerful than the friction.

Impatience with the speed of the program was to be expected, and in announcing some of the programs we were altogether too optimistic as to the date when benefit payments would go out. The tedious task of getting millions of contracts thoughtfully considered, signed, and then approved both locally and at Washington, took much longer than we thought it would. The mere physical job of handling that many contracts here at Washington, of auditing them and of getting out the checks, taxed our inventiveness to the utmost. By using the most ingenious machinery available—machinery which is uncanny in its transformation of punch-holes into names, addresses, and amounts—we were finally able to get the output of checks up to a maximum of 80,000 a day. But to do the job it required fifteen hundred people, plus a battery of comptometers and check-writing machines, working twenty-four hours a day.

The spectacle of all this going on in a room half a city block in area so impressed a Russian visitor last summer that he exclaimed, "Good Lord! This is a revolution!"

Any feeling that the adjustment machinery was fairly well under way, however, had to compete with some exceedingly disturbing situations in other sectors. The speculative spree in the markets during the early summer had ended with the customary reaction. Farm prices which had climbed sensationally ahead of other prices, now fell back, and their decline coincided with the Blue Eagle campaign and higher payrolls and prices in industry. From the Corn Belt came a chorus of protest at the rising retail prices and the declining farm prices.

Backseat drivers leaned over to tell us how to climb the mountain by starting in high. When we demurred, they did their best to get hold of the steering wheel and the gearshift.

The Farm Holiday folks in the Middle West were rarin' to go. A judge was jerked off his bench and confronted with a rope. A lawyer from an insurance company which was about to foreclose on an Iowa farm was tarred and feathered. Harassed debtors, kindly folk driven to desperation, were bound and determined to hold onto their farms and homes, law or no law. They would defy their creditors; they would defy the mysterious "system" which gave them unfairly low prices for their products by withholding food from the cities. They would insist on high prices by government fiat, and if the people in Washington couldn't hear their demands a thousand miles away, they would send a delegation of Governors on to the Capitol to make them hear.

These things happened, and many more. Sober citizens deplored the violence, but had to admit the depth of the grievance. Men whom I knew to be solid, hard-working farmers would dump milk in the ditch and defy the mortgage laws only when there seemed no other way to hold their farms and keep their families clothed and fed.

The Administration could not condone the violence and the defiance of law, but it could and did understand it. Every farmer in danger of foreclosure was invited to write, wire, or telephone to Washington in order to obtain the immediate assistance of the Farm Credit Administration. Farmers who had corn to sell were invited to apply for a Government loan at 45 cents a bushel on the farm, the corn was to be placed under seal for disposal in 1934. And finally, a corn-hog adjustment program involving $350,-000,000 in benefit payments during 1934 and 1935, was at last ready for launching.

By November, though a few reactionary politicians and metropolitan newspapers were doing their best to fan the flames, the Corn Belt rebellion had begun to subside. It was possible once more to appeal to men's minds, and to ask them, seriously, whether they were ready for the rigid regimentation implied in the demands for immediate price-fixing, or whether they would attempt the slower but surer program of adjusting supplies to demand as cotton, tobacco and wheat growers had already done, or, finally, whether they would join the Holiday movement and resort to violence.

If the reaction of an audience which filled the Des Moines Coliseum on Armistice Night was an indication, the people of the Corn Belt were through with the third course, mistrusted the first, and were ready to try the middle course.

The thunderstorm had cleared the air. It was possible then to explain the complicated corn-hog program, to recall why the emergency slaughter had to be followed up by an adjustment both in hog numbers and corn acreage in 1934, and to ask the help of thousands of volunteers in pushing this newest and hardest program over the top.

The emphasis we were putting on crop and livestock adjustment programs no doubt overshadowed, in the public mind, the efforts to get marketing agreements going. Some people, both within and without the AAA, thought we ought to forget the adjustment programs and concentrate on marketing agreements between producers and processors. We were willing to work as hard and as fast as we could on both, but most of us were unwilling to shove agreements through which we knew to be economically unsound and therefore unenforceable, and which gave processors and distributors significant rights without equally significant obligations. Whenever processors and dealers began to talk about price provisions based on their costs, we wanted the right to assure ourselves precisely what their costs were. When this right to examine books was denied us, there seemed no alternative but to postpone indefinitely the agreement involved. Several agreements got in that situation early in the game, and they are still there.

When Chester Davis succeeded George Peek as Administrator on December 15, Mr. Peek having accepted a position as Special Adviser to the President on Foreign Trade, some of our policies on agreements and licenses were undergoing severe strain. This was particularly true of certain milk marketing agreements.

We early ran into the pressure to set prices, by agreement, higher than consuming purchasing power warranted. When agreements and licenses are promulgated in the endeavor to fix a certain price, there is immediately an intense interest on the part of farmers, distributors, and consumers' representatives. If the price is set too high, the supply may be doubled, as was the case in a certain southern milkshed, while at the same time the consumption is decreased. Obviously, agreements of this sort are totally unenforceable. Prices in the different milksheds must be properly related to the butter, cheese, and by-products prices. And the total of all dairy product prices must be properly related to the income of city consumers, because it happens that the demand for dairy products goes up and down much more intimately with consumer purchasing power than is true of most other farm products. Dairy products are not exported in large volume, and therefore the theory of production control which applies to cotton,

wheat, hogs, and tobacco does not apply with equal force
to dairying.

The problem of getting satisfactory milk agreements
was further complicated by the necessity, under the law,
of giving distributors a long-sought protection against
price-cutting and various other unfair trade practices. Immediately that plunged us into long-standing conflicts between big distributors and little distributors, between huge
combines and small independents, between dealers who
delivered milk and stores which delivered it, and between
all of these and chain stores which sold on a cash and carry
basis. At times it was hard to see the woods of higher farm
prices for the trees of distribution. And always, there was
the consumer to consider.

We began to wonder whether we must, in order to help
the farmer, first settle the lusty feuds between big and little
distributors, or between chain stores and wagon delivery
dealers. At all events, we wanted to know whether, in order to give the farmers what they needed, we also had to
give the distributors everything they wanted.

Specifically, we were unwilling to permit the fixing of
retail prices to consumers until we knew the distributors'
costs and margins. We had to know whether the prices proposed were enforceable.

We were not surprised that many of the distributors
resisted such an examination, but it was a shock to find
certain important co-op leaders supporting the distributors
in their resistance. We knew, of course, that for years many
of the leaders had been compelled to work closely with
the distributors, for unless they played ball to some extent,
they could get nothing for the producers. But we hoped

the Adjustment Act had done away with the need for that sort of thing.

The attitude of the milkshed representatives was, "For God's sake do something, and do it quick!" Distributors and producer representatives combined to urge us to set up a complete price schedule first, slap on a license, and examine the books later and at leisure. They seemed willing to risk the possibility of prices too high to the consumer and of excessive profits to distributors. We were convinced that they did not give enough thought to the question of enforceability, but so long as the right to examine the books of the distributors was given us later on, we agreed, somewhat reluctantly, to put a few agreements into effect.

We discovered that we were being asked to license margins which in the past had meant decidedly good profits. It was not our duty to prevent profits, but we also felt that the Government could not be put in the position of licensing on a basis which practically guaranteed profits. We questioned whether the AAA should at once become an Interstate Commerce Commission for milk distributors.

The prices established and profits permitted in some of the agreements proved too high. Milk producers on the edges of the zone began to offer new competition, and small independent distributors began catering to consumer requests for cheaper milk. A flock of injunction proceedings finally convinced even the most optimistic that a new policy on marketing agreements must be adopted.

Early in January, accordingly, we announced a new policy. We declared that our first and principal concern to fix prices for milk producers at the highest level enforceable and economically sound, leaving the price to the consumer subject to competition. In some cases, we agreed, a maximum price to consumers might be specified. But as far as distributors' prices and margins were concerned, we did not see how the Government could permit them to be fixed unless the Government had authority to control distributors' profits.

What has been said of our experiences in trying to develop marketing agreements covering milk, is also more or less true of our experiences with agreements covering many special crops. From the long-time point of view, there may be much to be hoped for from the agreement and licensing sections of the Agricultural Adjustment Act. Unfortunately, thus far the expectations of benefits from agreements have been unreasonably great.

Agreements cannot soundly be used, for any length of time, to enable one section to benefit at the expense of another section, or one commodity to benefit at the expense of another commodity. Neither can the centralizing power of government be soundly used through these agreements to enable the distributing and processing concerns to increase their profits, while at the same time, the consumer is forced to pay more and the anti-trust laws are abrogated.

Agreements which merely deal with codes of fair practice, with uniform methods of marketing and grading, are in quite a different category from those which attempt to fix prices. The fixed-price agreements are the ones which are bound to lead to trouble unless they recognize continually the supply and demand situation, and the need of a formula giving justice to farmers, distributors, and consumers. The discovery of such a formula involves a long, slow process of mutual education.

A friend farming in Iowa has made it a practice to write me frequently about how things are going in his neighborhood. In January, 1934, came this word: "This is a great life we are living now, isn't it? I hardly know whether we are farming or not. Two days last week I was at Ames getting facts on the corn-hog plan. Monday night of this week I had a warehouse board meeting at Sac City; Tuesday night, night school at Sac City, and on Friday and Saturday, a county corn-hog meeting. Oh, well, there are better days coming."

Much the same word might have come, at one time or another since May 12, 1933, from men growing wheat in Kansas, or cotton in Texas, or tobacco in Kentucky. The adjustment programs, first approved by representatives of each industry, were being taken out to millions of individual growers for individual approval by well over a hundred thousand volunteer workers. They threw themselves into the necessary, if irritating, work of organization because they believed they saw a chance to lift themselves and their neighbors out of the mire of depression. They set up between three and four thousand county production control associations for the vital administrative problems involved in the adjustment programs, and they reawakened the countryside to the possibilities of economic self-government, and to the potentialities of the democratic process.

Producers of all but two of our major commodities were

having these experiences; for dairy products and beef cattle, no programs had been devised. Beef cattle, it is true, were omitted from the list of basic commodities in the Adjustment Act at the request of the industry, but the mounting number of cattle on farms and the declining prices made it likely that Congress would be asked to make beef cattle a basic commodity, and thereby subject to benefit payments—provided there was an adjustment program, and provided there were levied processing taxes to finance it. To many stockmen the benefit payments looked fine, but they had no stomach for the processing taxes. Under the original Agricultural Adjustment Act we could not make benefit payments without levying processing taxes.

Fluid milk producers, meanwhile, were fairly well absorbed in the marketing agreements, and in proposals for more rigid barriers around milksheds, while butter and cheese producers, according to some of their leaders, felt that their troubles would vanish if only stiff import duties could be levied on foreign fats and oils. They were still trying to find short-cuts to the Promised Land.

When we suggested that the dairy industry was headed for extreme trouble unless production was more nearly adjusted to market needs, particularly with the spring surplus coming along, the Washington representatives of the industry interposed one hurdle after another. They feared the effect of the processing tax, and they did not seem to look on the butter purchase program as a very binding obligation to pursue a production adjustment program, though that had been our understanding of it.

A compromise of some sort was essential, and it came in

an agreement to ask Congress for a special fund out of which benefit payments to dairymen and cattlemen could be paid, with the understanding that the Treasury would be reimbursed by processing taxes levied later on and at relatively low rates.

We had thought that devising an adjustment program for corn and hogs was difficult, but it was simple compared with the job now ahead of us.

With exports severely reduced, the surplus of corn and hogs was easily seen. Dairy products are rarely on an export basis, and per capita consumption of milk and butter and cheese has never been as high as nutrition experts think it ought to be. Nevertheless, dairymen could hardly be expected to give their products away. They had been doing too much of that for several months.

The only way to get prices up was to keep supplies at the level the market would take at a decent price. That was the logical approach to over-production. Aware that the dairy problem was also the result of underconsumption, we had already bought butter and distributed it to the unemployed, and we were prepared to do more of that sort of thing at the bidding of Congress. But further solution of the underconsumption problem would have to wait on higher purchasing power in the cities.

The program finally devised to adjust dairy production did not satisfy us, but it seemed to be the best we could get. It did not call for a serious cut in production, but for only enough to counteract the effects of the expected heavy flow of milk during the Spring pasture season. Each producer who signed a contract was free to devise his own method of making the reduction in milk and dairy products sold. Some might wish to dispose of their less productive cows; others might make the adjustment by feeding less intensively. To aid in the process, it was proposed to speed up the Government's existing campaign to eradicate bovine tuberculosis, and also to begin a new drive to clean out animals with Bang's disease.

We knew that this dairy program would not be worth the paper it was written on unless it had the approval of a large majority of producers. The other programs had enlisted from 75 to 95 per cent of the production; anything less than 75 per cent would have been hazardous. Accordingly, we decided to present the dairy plan at a series of regional meetings, and to estimate the sentiment for and against it.

The answer, we discovered, was "Yes" in the Middle West and "No" in the Northwest, with other regions registering less decisively. Some of those hostile to the plan released a flood of rather nasty propaganda, which may have influenced the decision somewhat, but in all probability not seriously. It was clear to us that there was not sufficient support to give the plan a fair chance, so it was promptly dropped.

As the thirteenth year neared its close, the machinery created by the Adjustment Act had to operate on increasingly difficult tasks. The 1934 cotton adjustment campaign, voluntarily inaugurated, was to be augmented by a compulsory adjustment scheme, involved in the Bankhead Act, and the tobacco growers were to experiment with a similar compulsory device in the Kerr Act. After sugar had been made a basic commodity, our efforts to help sugar producers deluged us with the past, present, and future difficulties of a commodity which has a peculiarly long list of such difficulties, and which plumped us squarely in the middle of a foreign trade problem, not to mention the matter of Philippine Independence.

On each of these subjects long, learned books could be written, and doubtless will be. I shall have to be content here with mentioning them in passing, referring the reader who desires more information to the publications of the Congress and the Department of Agriculture, and in particular to the first annual report of the Agricultural Adjustment Administration. There will be found the story of how three million farmers have contracted with the Government to adjust their production, and of how three-quarters of a million more are affected by marketing agreements on such items as milk, and citrus fruits, and walnuts, and gum turpentine. The factual pages of that annual report tell what the results have been in dollars and cents as well as in an improved supply and demand situation, insofar as that can be told at this time. It would be natural, I think, to show some pride in the fact that farm cash income rose 30 per cent during the first year the Adjustment Act was in effect, even granting that part of that increase should be credited to other Administration agencies.

I prefer to look upon this account of the twelve long years, and of the thirteenth year, as merely a catalogue of the hard facts our pioneers encountered as they set sail for a new world, as they tried to adjust old world psychology to new world ideals. Perhaps this last—this adjustment of old world psychology to new world ideals

—is more difficult and most important of all. For the great difficulty in designing social machinery at the moment is that it must be so fashioned as to operate in two worlds: it must utilize the habits and beliefs of our old individualistic pioneer world: simultaneously it must operate in a new world where powerful economic forces have made mincemeat of many established habits and beliefs. It is a little like trying to make an automobile travel on oats. We shall either have to learn how to convert oats into an acceptable fuel for automobiles, as it has been for horses, or we shall have to abandon it and try gasoline.

The ideals of the good life are relatively simple, but when it comes to working them out in practice the detailed decisions are endlessly perplexing. In approaching these myriad details, the all-important thing for younger minds to grasp is the need of courage, determination, and open-mindedness.

The plowing under of 10 million acres of cotton in August, 1933, and the slaughter of 6 million little pigs in September, 1933, were not acts of idealism in any sane society. They were emergency acts made necessary by the almost insane lack of world statesmanship during the period from 1920 to 1932.

Two important steps of advance toward the new world stand out clearly as a result of our first strenuous year of effort:—first, the idea of shaping productive forces to maintain a balance with a continually moving situation, had taken possession of the imagination of thousands of people: second, there had been formed what might be called a hierarchy of New England town meetings in the form of county and state production control associations, which provided in democratic fashion for carrying through as rapidly and justly as possible a comprehensive continent-wide, decentralized economic program.

Finally, important as the hard materialistic details may be, it is important to remember that the supremely important development is not any particular plan, but the willingness, from a social point of view, to modify the plan as often as necessary.

CHAPTER
XV

THE FOURTEENTH YEAR

IN THE fourteenth year we demonstrated that the Adjustment Act really was an adjustment act and not solely a reduction act.

Drought smote the land in 1934, the fourteenth year of the farm struggle. Never before in this country had there been anything like it. The fact that other nations in the northern hemisphere were similarly afflicted did not lessen our pain. For the drought created a new and gigantic relief problem; it compelled the Agricultural Adjustment Administration to face a situation in 1935 it did not expect to face until 1936 at the earliest; and it set in motion several imponderables—economic, social, political —the full effect of which none can foresee.

The first and most obvious consequence of the drought was to dispose of many of our accumulated surpluses. What the AAA had planned to do over two or three years, the drought did—except for cotton and tobacco—in one. What farmers in the drought area will remember, however, is that production control by drought carried no benefit payments, adhered to no modest 15 or 20 per cent reduction of each man's acreage, but ruthlessly and blindly struck right and left. They did not see, in drought, any-thing remotely resembling social machinery for the com-mon good.

And yet, by the combined efforts of man and nature, the domestic wheat surplus was nearly wiped out; hog supplies were brought down to normal; cattle and sheep supplies, because of government purchases in drought areas, were on the way to normal; and corn supplies promised to be at the reduced level required by a reduced hog and cattle population.

Thus in a haphazard, drastic way burdensome farm supplies were temporarily adjusted to demand, but the adjustment by drought was disastrous to millions. Of fur-ther consequences of the drought, we can only guess. One effect may be to stiffen consumer resistance to advancing food prices. A second may be to threaten a new cycle of farm surpluses.

Retail food prices in 1935 are likely to be 10 or 15 per cent above the first half of 1934, studies made at the mo-ment of writing suggest. Total living costs, however, should not be more than 5 or 10 per cent higher, since rent, clothing, and other items are not affected by drought. That would bring the index of living costs up to 80 or 85 per cent of 1923 costs.

Most of these increased food prices will probably occur in dairy and poultry products, in response to drought-shortened pasture and forage. A material increase is also to be expected in meat prices, directly as a result of heavy slaughtering for drought relief and of the corn-hog adjust-ment program, and indirectly as a result of feed shortage. While it is true that neither the feed shortage nor the higher dairy or poultry prices can be attributed to the AAA, opponents of agricultural adjustment will try to pin responsibility on AAA, regardless.

The possibility that the drought may threaten a new cycle of farm surpluses is perhaps the toughest possibility of all to face. Most farmers, seeing their crops drying up under the blazing sun, did not visualize in the summer of 1934 that the high prices growing out of the drought would of themselves bring about a new cycle of surpluses.

But if there is no control—I do not say reduction—of corn acreage in 1935, it is fairly certain that there will be a great expansion in acreage and a probable total yield in excess of 2,700,000,000 bushels. In the past, years of low per-acre yields have almost invariably been followed by years of relatively high per-acre yields. With livestock supplies cut down, a crop of 2,700,000,000 bushels of corn would mean a surplus of several hundred million bushels. Low corn prices and high livestock prices in the late fall of 1935 would initiate an expansion in livestock production beginning in 1936 that would prove disastrous within three or four years.

As for wheat, the extremely short crops of 1933 and 1934 lifted Chicago prices 15 cents above Liverpool, thus making exports impossible except by subsidy. If there is no control of wheat acreage in 1935, average weather will result in a production of from 750 to 950 million bushels. This would increase the carryover of wheat as of July 1, 1936, to somewhere between 270 and 420 million bushels. American wheat prices would then assume their "normal" relationship to Liverpool, or, in other words, about 25 cents a bushel under the 1934 relationship. It is entirely possible, therefore, that a single year of release from agricultural adjustment would drive wheat prices to the American farmer down to 40 cents a bushel.

In May and June of 1934 the AAA began to overhaul its program with the drought in mind. Members of the Administration appeared before committees in Congress to call attention to the way in which the spring drought had already cut down pasture and hay crops, thus making inevitable the death on the range of millions of cattle unless arrangements could be made to slaughter and can them at central markets for relief purposes. Our presentation, and that of the Federal Emergency Relief Administration, apparently convinced Congress of the need to appropriate over half a billion dollars for drought relief. Some Congressmen thought this sum altogether too much, but knowing the tendency of drought to breed on itself, we pointed out the possibility of a burning summer drought following the burning spring. We wanted to be prepared for the worst.

Because the spring drought had cut down pasture and hay crops, the AAA in June issued regulations permitting the land contracted out of production to be used for forage crops. As a result, the total output of forage in 1934 was millions of tons greater than if the contracted land had been planted to its customary wheat, corn, or cotton. The corn loans, by keeping 270 million bushels of corn under seal on farms, out of the hands of speculators, probably saved more than 30 million bushels for the emergency. The reduction of 28 per cent in the 1934 spring pig crop, in line with the corn-hog adjustment program, reduced the livestock demand for corn by at least 300 million bushels. Against these savings, there must be put the corn acreage reduction, representing a reduction in total output of about 250 million bushels. The total effect of the AAA operations, therefore, was to reduce the supply of hogs to domestic consumption and at the same time make more corn available for cattle, sheep, and poultry than would have been otherwise at hand.

Whether these facts would be recognized by farmers and the general public, and remembered in any appraisal of the AAA was not so certain. The fact that benefit payments were the only income for hundreds of thousands of drought-afflicted farmers did seem to be widely understood and approved, and the crop insurance feature of the adjustment programs therefore had some chance of being regarded in the same light as unemployment insurance. The purchase of millions of cattle as drought relief, and ultimately as a source of meat for the unemployed, was also, I believe, generally approved.

Nevertheless, it remained possible that an appeal to prejudice could wreck the whole program. In the summer of 1934, a good many people began to say that since all surpluses were now out of the way, or soon would be, the need for the Adjustment Administration was over. They looked on the AAA, of course, as a reduction rather than an adjustment administration. It has been my view from the first that the surplus does not consist merely of surplus bushels and bales, but of those 50 million extra acres of plowland which has been producing stuff for sale to foreign countries. We must either keep those acres out of production, or lower tariffs sufficiently to create additional foreign purchasing power for the product of those acres.

In a sense the drought revealed how useful it is to have a nation's agriculture on an export basis. When we were exporting, year after year, a fifth of our wheat, a half of our packing-house lard, and so on, we had no fear that drought or flood could ever menace our food supply. It would only be necessary to keep more at home, export less. The exports were our elastic reserve.

But with foreign markets gone, at least temporarily, that reserve piled up at home and crushed our producers with the resulting low prices. Carryovers had to be worked down to normal. The normal wheat carryover, for instance, is about 120 million bushels. But that "normal" is no longer adequate, if we are not to produce 200 million bushels in addition for export, making a total of over 300 million bushels to fall back on when necessary in years of short crops. The new "normal," if we are to be free of any danger of food shortage, has to be well above the old.

How to maintain the increased carryover without having it depress prices unduly,—that becomes the problem. In May of 1934 we began thinking about it. In speeches throughout the country I thought it wise to mention the possibility and ask for criticisms and suggestions. The reader will find the idea discussed in some detail in the latter part of Chapter XVII, "Smoothing Out the Cycles."

Of course, the drought had not been anticipated when the 1934 AAA plans were being formulated. As it worked out in the end, however, more feed was available in 1934, in proportion to the livestock, than would have been available if production control programs had not been in operation. These programs brought about an orderly adjustment in hog, cattle, and sheep numbers, and a net increase in forage, pasture, and hay crop plantings. As a result, agriculture came through the season with about six per cent more grain per grain-consuming animal, and with about 17 per cent more hay per hay-and-pasture consuming animal than would otherwise have been available. Without the programs, the production of feed grains would have been somewhat larger. But livestock numbers would have been much larger. Without the Adjustment programs, the volume of grain available per grain consuming animal unit would have been about .52 tons, as compared with .55 tons that will actually be available. Encouragement given by the programs to hay production will make the current hay supply about 13 per cent greater than it otherwise would have been. In the case of hogs particularly, the adjustment programs show a substantial benefit. Hog production would have been much larger had the programs not been put into effect, and the enforced liquidation of surplus stock at very low prices would have involved severe loss. The hog programs averted disordered and expensive last minute adjustments. Without the livestock buying programs, cattle and sheep would have fallen below the point at which they can offset marketing costs.

Early in the summer of 1934 it began to be plain that the 1935 adjustment programs would have to be radically different from those of 1934, for the need had changed. Even though there was only one chance in a hundred of another drought coming along in 1935, it seemed wise to allow for the possibility, now that excessive carryovers had been cut down, and to relax our acreage control pro-

grams, while at the same time maintaining sufficient organization to prevent the creation of new price-depressing
surpluses. While tariffs remain high, and foreign trade
low, there is no other acceptable course for American Agriculture.

CHAPTER
XVI

WE TAX BREAD AND MEAT

THE fuel which drives our present machinery for adjusting agriculture to changed conditions is money, largely derived from processing taxes levied on farm products. In 1934 a few powerful interests determined to do away with processing taxes. There are many who could be easily persuaded. Undoubtedly processing taxes can be made even more unpopular to the more thoughtless as farm prices move higher.

All people hate the idea of taxes. The subject sounds dull and horrid. Most people feel that they are paying more than their fair share of taxes and that other people are paying less.

Food taxes are hated worse than others. When we put a tax of thirty cents a bushel on wheat in July of 1933, it was the same as putting a tax of one-half cent on every loaf of bread. Of course, this isn't so very much. But even though it means only about two dollars per family a year, plus another two dollars for the tax on flour otherwise used, the women who do the buying became a little uneasy. Later, we put a tax of two and a quarter cents on each pound of live hog marketed. This amounts, on the average, to a tax of around seven dollars a year, for each family, on hog meats. Processing taxes on cotton and tobacco run the total contribution of the average family to around twenty dollars a year.

The money so raised is paid to the families producing export crops on condition that they will raise less of them. The reduced output after a year or two will raise the prices still further and it will be very easy to arouse a great outcry in the cities of the United States against the processing tax.

Long ago, of course, there should have been a far greater outcry about the cost of high tariffs. Fundamentally the tariff and the processing tax are twins. There are, however, three important differences: (1) the processing tax is admittedly an emergency measure, whereas the tariff has been with us for generations; (2) the total cost of the tariff is apparently many times that of the processing tax; (3) the ad valorem rates of the Smoot-Hawley tariff on many important items are far higher than the rates of the processing tax.

In saying that the total cost of the tariff is apparently many times that of the processing tax, I have no exact statistical measurement in mind. It is almost impossible to get such a measurement, so complex is the problem of tariff costs and effects. But it stands to reason that if a tariff did not succeed in keeping domestic prices higher than world prices, or in some other way reducing competition from abroad, domestic interests would not fight for it. Under normal conditions domestic prices of many highly protected products undoubtedly may rise by the full amount of the tariff.

To all intents and purposes the processing tax is the farmer's tariff. It is the only effective form of tariff for producers of export crops, prices for which are determined on a world market. If America is to remain on a highly protectionist basis, therefore, the processing tax form of tariff protection, or its equivalent, would seem to be no more than just.

Nevertheless, all classes of society instinctively dislike the processing tax. It is easy to prejudice the farmers against it because enemies argue that in some cases the processing tax results in lower prices for the product taxed and this is felt by the farmers before the benefit payments are returned to them. Moreover, even though the benefit payments are returned to them, farmers dislike the processing tax because its purpose is to enable them to reduce acreage, and it has been their custom in the past to produce as much as possible of everything that they felt moved to produce.

Railroad men instinctively question the desirability of a processing tax because the money is used to reduce output and the reduced output means less tonnage and, therefore, less income to railroads. Commission men who handle farm products at Chicago, Omaha, and other central markets, dislike reduced output because it lowers the total volume of their commissions, which are based on the units handled and not on percentage of value. Millers, packers, cotton spinners, and other processors dislike the processing tax because they have to collect it and they feel that small processors and certain farmers may be bootlegging processed goods, evading the tax.

The consumer dislikes the tax because of the increased

cost. Of course, so far as the consumer is concerned, it should be said that he is protected in the law by the provision that whenever the price of a commodity rises to a point where he is paying as large a percentage of his dollar for it as he did before the war, then the tax is not to be levied the following year. In other words, after agricultural product prices reach a fair point, the tax is taken off. But the consumer dislikes the tax just the same.

It is to be expected that strong efforts will be made to get rid of the processing taxes by every Congress from now on. Processing taxes will be denounced vigorously in the Congressional campaigns of the even-numbered years. In these campaigns in certain localities, farmers will be told that they pay the processing taxes, while in the cities the consumers will be convinced that they pay them.

The processing taxes are like Horatio at the Bridge. They are saving the situation until the American people are ready to take decisive action.

I trust that farmers fully realize the great import of the processing tax as part of this Administration's effort to give unprotected and unorganized groups a fairer share of the national income. For the first time in our history we have created a mechanism, the AAA, which gives six million individual farmers a concerted voice, and bargaining power. Similarly, the NIRA provided, through paragraph 7a, for the right of labor to organize and to make the voices of millions of laborers more effectively heard, in terms of wages and hours. Laborers all over the country are sensing the meaning of their extended right to bargain collectively with employers under rules laid down by the centralizing power of the government. In some industries they are even going to extremes to assure themselves of a fuller utilization of the social and economic privilege which the country, in a mood of fair play, entrusted to them. Farmers fortunately do not have to resort to strikes to assure themselves of the benefits of the collective power embodied in the Agricultural Adjustment Act. They should, however, be just as zealous in their desire to retain that centralizing power which is now theirs and to utilize it in the interest of agriculture, and in the interest of all groups concerned.

I would not mind seeing the processing tax and acreage control abolished in 1936 if we have something better to take its place. But unless we have built up greatly increased foreign purchasing power by reducing tariffs, or unless we start loaning money outside the United States to enable foreign nations to buy our surplus, I am afraid that dropping the processing tax and acreage control in 1936 would result, with the ordinary run of weather, in a repetition within a few years of the 1932 situation.

In saying this I realize quite well that during the first year or two after the removal of the processing taxes, the result might seem quite happy, indeed. In the case of a product like hogs, I would anticipate that a sudden removal of the processing tax might result in some increase in cash prices. If this comes at the same time that there is a reduced production resulting from the previous production control, the outcome would be to cause unthinking farmers to say, "Isn't it fine without that processing tax? Look how much better off we are without it!"

It is exceedingly important now to weigh all the possible

substitutes for a processing tax. If no substitute is provided, and foreign purchasing power has not been increased by reduced tariffs, I am very much afraid that farm product prices within three years will be down again to a point where they will buy only half as much city products as they should buy in order to give this country a balanced prosperity. No one wants a repetition of 1932.

The only possible processing tax substitutes I can think of which will avoid the 1932 situation are as follows:

1. Raise the money for acreage control by means of a general sales tax.
2. Raise the money for acreage control by means of higher income taxes.
3. Control production by compulsion, giving each farmer a quota and taxing each farmer if he markets more than that quota.
4. Use a combination of stabilization purchases and loans to farmers on commodities in years of large crops and low prices. Given an initial capital of a billion dollars, perhaps more, a government agency might offer loans above the market price much as has been done with the 1933 corn crop, provided (a) that borrowers agree to reduce acreage by some specified amount the following year, and (b) that enough farmers accept loans to make the plan effective on supply.
5. Drop production control entirely but use instead marketing control with each farmer given his prorated share of the domestic market at a fixed domestic price and with the surplus flowing into the foreign markets at whatever the world market price may be. This is known as the "Pro-rate two-price system."
6. Drop production control and restore foreign purchasing power by loaning approximately $500,000,000 annually to foreign nations.

7. Drop production control and restore foreign purchasing power by lowering tariffs sufficiently to cause imports to exceed exports by at least $500,000,000 annually.

8. Use some combination of these different methods.

I have thought quite a bit about each of these and I am not convinced that any one of them will make the American people as a whole any happier than the processing tax does now. Let us examine the other methods a little further:

1. A sales tax on all manufactured products at the rate of about 1¼ per cent, assuming present sales levels, would provide about $500,000,000, which is about the amount collected annually now by the processing taxes on wheat, cotton, tobacco, corn, and pork products. The present processing taxes represent on the average a tax of about 30 per cent on those commodities. The processors paying this tax therefore strongly urge that it would be more equitable, since the benefits are spread amongst all classes of society, to spread the costs by means of a low tax on many products rather than by a high tax on a few products.

If a fund of $500,000,000 a year were raised by a sales tax on all manufactured products, it would be possible to approach the agricultural problem somewhat differently than the present Adjustment Act requires. The present Act forces all the people concerned with the product in trouble—wheat, for example—to think about the nature and magnitude of the trouble, because the fact that the processing tax is measured by the discrepancy between the market price and parity price; and the money for straightening out the trouble is obtained from the consumers of that particular product.

If a large sum of money were available from a general sales tax, the agricultural problem could be approached from a more general standpoint, which might or might not be desirable. In the case of the feed grain problem in relation to livestock, I can see advantàges. Instead of thinking about the plowland in the Corn Belt as divided up among corn and barley and oats and hay, and instead of being troubled about a program for each product, it would be possible to enter into a program for reducing, by a certain percentage, the land under plow; and leave it to the contracting farmers to make their own adjustments between crops on the plowland and livestock fed such crops.

A serious disadvantage of large funds raised by a general sales tax is the political pressure that would surely be brought to bear by the representatives of the different commodities, each endeavoring to get a share of the money. Some definite method of measurement would have to be provided by law to protect the program against such pressure.

2. The proposal to resort to higher income taxes is also open to some of the same objections. Most economists look on income taxes as a sounder source of revenue than sales taxes. To that extent this substitute for the processing tax seems better. In normal years it seems possible to derive far more revenue from income taxes than we did, for example, in 1926-30, when the total collected annually was more than a billion dollars under the higher-rate years, 1920 and 1921.

From certain quarters there might come the objection that income tax revenue should be devoted more exclusively to such general social purposes as social insurance, scientific research, unemployment insurance, and the educational activities of the Federal Government.

But the most immediate and potent objection, I have no doubt, would come from the big income taxpayers. They still have so much influence in Congress that radically higher income taxes are not likely to be voted.

3. We might control production by compulsion. That is the method provided in the Bankhead and Kerr Acts, affecting cotton and tobacco this year. Personally, I dislike the method, and I think most farmers, once they have tried it, will dislike it. If I am wrong about the attitude of farmers; if the Bankhead and Kerr Acts prove effective in the crop year 1934-5, then I should not be surprised to see the method spread slowly to the control of other products. But the administrative difficulties of fixing and enforcing quotas for millions of individual farmers are appalling, and the opportunities for bootlegging and cheating are obviously great. My inclination is to look upon this substitute for the processing tax as a last resort. It is also to be remembered that the Bankhead and Kerr Acts this year are not substitutes for the processing tax and the benefit payment, but are merely superimposed on the voluntary adjustment programs.

4. The proposal to make commodity loans in years of large crops and low prices runs the risk that any stabilization effort involves. Several years of low prices might strain the exchequer seriously. The Farm Board experience comes to mind, but with this exception: Unlike the Farm Board, it would be possible under this plan to grant loans only upon agreement to reduce acreage the follow-

ing year. Even in time of depression, excessively low prices might thereby be avoided by a supply reasonably well adjusted to demand. We would have, of course, to draw from the Treasury the initial capital; so this proposal is only a partial substitute for some form of taxation. Perhaps the most difficult obstacle would be the influence on market prices of these commodities, under loan. A way would have to be found to release commodities without seriously depressing prices.

5. There seems to be a growing interest in this pro-rate two-price system. In effect, however, it is a revival of interest in many farm relief schemes discarded during the past dozen years.

The effect of the two-price system would not differ from the effect of the processing tax, as far as the consumer is concerned. He would have to pay just as much for bread and cloth and pork as he pays now. The administrative difficulties would be greater than with the processing tax, for the government would be charged completely to supervise every processing and marketing operation, and forced to determine whether products were for domestic or for foreign consumption.

An expansion of acreage and production might be expected in time under the stimulus of higher domestic prices. The surpluses of this expansion would go out on the world markets at the lower world price. This usually constitutes "dumping." New Zealand would object strenuously to having our butter sold in England on that basis; Australia, Canada, and Argentina would object to wheat sales on that basis; Denmark would say unkind things about our pork exports. And so it would go until distress

forced us to adopt restrictive measures. Nevertheless, I
have included the pro-rate two-price idea in this list. It is
likely to have considerable support.

6. Restoring foreign purchasing power by loaning large
sums of money abroad is the method we followed until
1930. It is the logical procedure for a great creditor nation,
provided—and this is the indispensable provision—that our
debtors are permitted to pay their obligations in the only
way most of them can pay us—in goods and services. That
involves an increase in imports of goods and services
roughly corresponding to the total of our loans abroad. If
that indispensable provision is adhered to, the loaning
policy is basically sound. Otherwise, it is economic suicide.

7. The proposal I favor as probably the soundest partial
substitute for the processing tax is this:

Restore foreign purchasing power for our exports by
importing half a billion dollars worth of goods above the
amount we now import. This policy encourages each nation to produce what each is best equipped to produce,
with resultant lower costs of production the world over,
lower costs of living, and higher standards of living for all
classes. I have explored this course elsewhere in this book.
At the moment it is enough to point out that the goal of
increased imports can be reached only gradually, and that
political difficulties in the way seem at times insuperable.

8. A combination of some of the above substitutes for
the processing tax might be practical. Obviously an increase of $200,000,000 in imports in excess of exports
would be easier to obtain than a larger amount, and the
elimination of 25 million acres from export production
would seem less objectionable to many than the present

program. Precisely which combination would best satisfy our people is anybody's guess just now. An answer should be forthcoming in 1935 or 1936 at the latest.

To have the question go by default would wreck the adjustment machinery and put hope of balance among our major producing groups back where it was in 1921. This is something for not only farmers to think about. It concerns us all. The processing tax, it is true, has in effect been the farmer's tariff, and for that reason alone farmers, with the world as it is, would be foolish to give it up without getting an acceptable substitute, for the longer pull.

FOURTH SECTION

UNTROD PATHS

CHAPTER
XVII

SMOOTHING OUT THE CYCLES

THE tendency for the majority of men to run excitedly in one direction for five, ten, fifteen or twenty years, and then turn around and run in the other, causes cycles of maladjustment which add greatly to human uncertainty and suffering.

The longest cycles of which we have historic record are those dealing with civilization itself. Judging from the past, we may say that a civilization ordinarily is born, expresses itself, and sinks into darkness in 1500 or 2000 years. Petrie the Egyptologist and Spengler the German philosopher, in analyzing the cycles of civilizations assume that, culturally speaking, the United States is part of the European civilization which found its birth about the year 1000.

During the first 800 or 900 years civilizations customarily express themselves in religious architecture, sculpturing, painting, music and philosophy. The somewhat vague idealism of philosophy leads to the more concrete investigations of science, and science brings about the more definite control of nature. This produces wealth. Wealth eventually saps the vitality of the earlier cultural ideas, and the bonds of political unity. After five hundred years of wealth there comes an increasing tendency for people to say, "What's the use?" Then a barbarous and more virile people, formerly under the domination of the center of civilization and formerly respecting it, overthrow the old center. A period of unrest ensues. The different races are fused. New ideas begin to take form and serve eventually as the seeds of the next culture.

Toward the close of the Græco-Roman civilization, from the time of Cæsar onward, it is interesting to read of the increasing drift of people into the cities as wealth increased. Here they formed guilds or trade unions. Many efforts were made, often with the help of the government, to fix wages and prices. Life in the cities was made more attractive than on the Italian farms. The city population wanted cheap bread. So the Italian wheat farmer was sacrificed for the benefit of the wheat farmer of Northern Africa. A permanently unemployed class developed in the cities. They felt that the government owed them free bread and entertainment at the circuses. When the funds did not exist to take care of unemployment either by public building or by bread and circuses, it was always possible to draft the unemployed into the army. This served simultaneously to take care of the unemployment problem, and to replenish national funds by a drive for plunder against a neighboring region.

There is sufficient likeness between the Græco-Roman civilization and our own to make us consider to what extent we are in a period somewhat similar to that of Augustus Cæsar. To what extent are we cutting the firm base out from under us? We have abused our soil and our agricultural population much as the Romans did. To what extent are we making it possible for the cities to suck the lifeblood of the countryside? To what extent are we allowing certain sections of the population to use the centralizing power of government to set prices and wages in a way which will distort the balance between farm and city?

With modern machinery, modern science, and the insight obtainable in our modern universities, there is no necessary compulsion for this civilization to follow the rhythms of the past. Nevertheless, attitudes taken by our city people, both in industry and labor, have been such during the past twenty years as seriously to alarm the more thoughtful farm leadership. Some are beginning to wonder if there may not be some force in human nature itself which causes a civilization to go through certain successive stages, and finally after control over Nature has created wealth, to enter into the period of decline.

Did Roman leaders in the time of the Cæsars speculate on the causes of the decline of the ancient Egyptian and Persian civilizations? Probably not—and to that extent we may have a decided and determining advantage over the Romans. We have the opportunity to profit by their mistakes and prevent convulsive upset.

In studying the cycles of civilizations, it is interesting to trace changing attitude toward money and banks. Early in the civilization, while the agricultural element is still dominant, prices are low. They are low because of the shortage of the precious metals and the credit based thereon and because, in a primitive state, demand flows slowly. The self-sufficient individual has few demands. Later on, the supply of precious metals increases greatly.

Credit mechanisms are discovered to enable each unit of precious metal to go much further in performing the work of money. Men then fall under the money illusion, which makes it possible for a while to coordinate human efforts over wide areas of space and time, but only with severe periodic shocks when it is discovered that serious miscalculations have been made.

In our own civilization it is interesting to note that prices 700 years ago were apparently about one-fifth what they have been in recent years. A pronounced and sudden rise came between 1530 and 1650. Enormous quantities of precious metals found their way from the new to the old world at that time. During the following century, prices on the whole tended slightly upward. Another pronounced rise associated with various wars, occurred between 1740 and 1815. This was followed by a protracted decline to 1890. Strong recessions took place after the Napoleonic and the recent World War. It has been necessary again and again to reduce the weight of precious metal behind the unit of currency in the different countries, in order that contracts might be met. The pressure of the increasing burden of debt over the centuries seems to be on the side of continually rising prices with intermediate recessions of from twenty to fifty years duration.

The battle between debtors and creditors as they try to influence the money mechanism in line with their prejudices is almost as significant as the battle between farmers and city people. A truly enduring civilization will discover how to meet both problems and thus achieve stability. Upsets and collapses came again and again upon ancient civilizations because they played the game with the dice loaded to favor particular groups.

There appears throughout the history of human affairs what is called the "cycle of the generations." Each generation tends in some measure to be the opposite of the one before. It sees some of the mistakes of the old people and tries to avoid them. But in avoiding the mistakes of the fathers it may fall into the errors of the grandfathers.

Observe, for instance, the tendency for a serious war to come every other generation. No generation which has seen a great war and the terrible economic after-effects is likely to permit such a frightful thing to happen twice. The generation born in the shadow of the great war may, also, be so impressed as to throw its influence for many years against such disaster. But memories, especially when passed on by tradition, grow dim; and there are certain provocative forces growing out of peace long continued which all too readily lead to war again.

In this tendency of great wars to recur every fifty years we perceive a suggestion of a cycle of the generations. Again we see it from the agricultural viewpoint. When agricultural prices have been rising faster than other prices, it is necessary for the tendency to continue for twenty or thirty years before there is sufficient expansion of all kinds of agricultural output to reverse the trend.

Over the entire world agricultural prices began to rise about 1896. They continued to rise until the end of the world war. During the five years before the war there was much talk of farm product prices being relatively higher than the wages of labor. There was clamor in the city press. In America the abbreviation "H.C.L." (for high cost of living) became widely familiar. Industrial leaders of England and Germany found it increasingly difficult to satisfy their laboring men, and they reached out with an increasing desperation for world markets.

When the war ended the situation was completely reversed. Farmers who had lived through the rising prices of 1896 to 1919 had developed a psychology poorly adapted to meeting the difficulties of the continually falling prices from 1920 onward. After a major war it seems to take twenty or thirty years of low prices to convince farmers that the good old days are not just around the corner all the time.

In the '60's and early '70's of the last century there were several great wars which temporarily stimulated the world demand for farm products. After these wars ended, in the early '70's, farm products prices throughout the entire civilized world declined until 1896. This long and harsh decline stimulated migration to the cities. Country blood entered into the expansion of factories, and thus laid the groundwork for the world wide industrial push which began in 1896.

When a man once starts farming he does not quit easily. He intends to make it a life work, and if his resources permit, he will cling to that farm year after year in spite of bad weather and bad markets. He always expects the situation to change. With his children it is different. They can see that their father is up against an impossible situation. They survey the alternative opportunities and decide what they would like to do, rather than live under the situation that has caused their parents so much grief. They get out; and this contributes to the tendency for farm prices to go up faster than the prices of other things for twenty or thirty years at a time, and then remain below a just relationship with the prices of other things for twenty or thirty years.

We had never had anything quite like the World War. We have never had anything like the situation thereafter. But it would still seem that the exceedingly low prices prevailing over the great agricultural regions of the world since 1919 would normally result in sufficient worldwide discouragement on the part of farmers and their children, so that the effect, if left untended, would become apparent about ten years hence in a worldwide food shortage.

This shortage might, of course, come sooner if bad weather reinforces the tendency of the cycle of the generations. Perhaps it may be delayed or prevented entirely by appropriate governmental action. If a serious food shortage does come, it can easily result in such dissension among the laboring men and others in the cities as leads to war or an internal revolution.

It seems wise and necessary, therefore, to moderate or prevent that excessive violence which has come in the past from the ungoverned swing of the cycle of the generations. This we are attempting to do by the Agricultural Adjustment Act. We are trying to produce continuously a supply and demand situation which will get farmers their normal share of the national income. Curtailment was necessary, during the first two years of the Act, because of the enormous carryover which has been built up, beginning in 1928. In the event of normal weather in 1935 and 1936, the acreage control program should be continued for sometime. The lesson of the cycle of the generations remains for the long pull, the same:—There probably will be serious food shortage over the entire world beginning sometime during the next ten or fifteen years, and that the shortage once definitely started will continue for a number of years, with an intensity varying, of course, with the weather.

In 1930, 1931, 1933 and 1934 there were serious droughts and unusual temperatures over extended areas of the earth. Most students of weather cycles think we now are nearing the close of a dry period which began about 1908. They expect an increased rainfall, especially in northwestern United States, may gradually and spasmodically begin sometime within the next two or three years. There are some, however, who feel that we may be in for a number of further years of drought. In any event we should not take undue chances.

If, as a result of the lost foreign markets which will not be returned to us until we import greatly increased quantities of goods, we find it necessary to reduce our domestic crop acreage, one year with another, by 30 million or more; and if we are no longer to produce any great quantity of food for export, may it not be the part of wisdom to hold in storage much larger quantities of agricultural produce than we have formerly considered normal?

We have before us as a warning the experience of the Farm Board. We do not want to build up these adequate stocks in such a way as will continually depress prices and damage the farmer. We want the strong hand of the government in control of these stocks, but the plan must be such that no mere political attack can dislodge it. Furthermore, the question marks that traders in the Farm Board days had on that plan must be removed, by the very nature of this one.

The combined experience of the Farm Board, the Agricultural Adjustment Administration, and the Commodity Credit Corporation gives us the outlines of a plan, philosophically not greatly different from that of Joseph, in Bible days, or of the Confucians in ancient China. They, too, sought a constantly normal granary.

We first began to think about it seriously in respect to corn in the spring of 1934. The winter before, our Commodity Credit Corporation had loaned farmers 45¢ a bushel, a little above the market price, on 270 million bushels of corn. The loan had been made without recourse. That is to say, if the price was below 45¢ a bushel in the late summer of 1934 when the loan came due, the government would take the corn in satisfaction of the loan. In a way it was, "Tails I win, heads you lose," so far as the farmer was concerned. He could be sure of the 45¢ a bushel for his corn, and in case the market went up, as it did go up in July of 1934, he could sell for 50¢ a bushel and take a profit.

This program of loaning above the market without recourse would ordinarily be unjustifiable. But the situation in the fall of 1933 was such that the program was wise, especially since it required the farmer receiving a loan to agree to participate in the 1934 curtailment program.

Events justified our course. If there had not been a serious drought in the summer of 1934, the government might have come into possession of more than two hundred million bushels of corn. We gave this possibility very serious consideration in the spring and early summer of 1934. Our conclusion was, that in case the government did come into possession of this enormous quantity of corn, which it had sealed and stored on the farms, the government could use government-owned corn, in lieu of cash as a benefit payment to farmers who would curtail their corn acreage by a specified amount in 1935. In brief, we could prevent burdensome corn supplies from accumulating, and the corn price from breaking unduly, by using corn supplies, accumulated in years of large crops, to reduce the acreage the following year.

We then began to develop in our minds the idea that the government, through the Commodity Credit Corporation, should not loan money at the market price or above the market price except in years of large crops or undue price demoralization; and that during the following year or the year thereafter, any surplus accumulated as a result of loaning without recourse could be used effectively in restoring a fair price, by the means I have described: that is, offer it in lieu of benefit payments to farmers cooperating in acreage control.

We felt then that we were beginning to perfect the ancient Chinese idea of the "constantly normal granary." Government financing of large corn supplies could thus be used to stabilize the corn price at a fair level, to keep it from going unduly low in years of low price and unduly high in years of high price. A more uniform corn supply and a more uniform corn price would stabilize the quantity of fat livestock coming on the market. And the whole thing would be economically sound and safe, because the money would be loaned without recourse only to farmers who would agree to curtail their acre ge in case the stored supplies became burdensome. The objective—a more uniform supply and a more uniform price for corn from year to year—is a permanent foundation of stability under the livestock industry which in turn would contribute enormously to the stability of the entire business structure in the United States.

The problem of loaning without recourse on wheat is somewhat different. It is more difficult to loan with safety on wheat stored on the farm than on corn so stored, because the facilities for safe farm wheat storage are not adequate over large areas. Personally, I am convinced that a little scientific technical intelligence applied to the problem of farm wheat storage would remedy this situation. If so, it would then be quite feasible to loan government money on wheat stored on the farm. If such farm storage facilities for wheat can be devised it should be done, because of the psychological effect on the farmer. He appreciates the reality of the surplus if it is there before him. He is in a position to see the surplus more definitely as a part of the entire adjustment program when it piles up there, before his eyes. It remains, however, possible to loan on wheat stored in the local elevator, or in terminal elevators, if adequate farm storage can not be practically provided.

Our experience in loaning without recourse on cotton indicated the advisability of storing away from the farm in the better types of warehouses. It would seem that by use of government loans without recourse to cotton farmers who agree to accept cotton in lieu of cash whenever acre-

age reduction is necessary, we can regulate over a period
of years the price and production of cotton in such a way
as satisfies the southern farmer, the cotton spinner and the
consumer.

The outstanding danger I see in this program is a tendency continually to push the government loan higher, no
matter what the situation may be. In the fall of 1933 we
loaned 10¢ a pound on cotton. By July of 1934 requests
were coming in that a new cotton loan program be established for the purpose of loaning 15¢ a pound on cotton.
We settled at 12¢. If we had loaned 15¢ a pound on cotton
and escaped crucial trouble, the request would come for
20¢ a pound in 1935, and so on indefinitely until the crash.

If farmers, pushing on, get city people on the run as a
result of borrowing the centralizing power of government
they will be just as shortsighted and neglectful of their
own eventual interests as their urban brethren of the
immediate past. For my part, I am convinced that the concept of an ever-normal granary can not be satisfactorily
administered unless those in positions of power determinedly hold to the concept of a harmonious continuing
balance, and resist at all times the pressure of shortsighted
local or occupational groups.

Such a program should have the support of thoughtful
people in both present parties, and they must insist that
the plan be administered and developed from one administration to the next without regard to regional or occupational politics.

If we are ever to govern and manage, scientifically, as a
people, the short-time cycles, it is most important that the

effect of unusual weather be well understood. Extreme drought, such as that of 1934, results in a vast reduction of grain and an advance in prices which temporarily bring about a surging increase in livestock sent to market. A year or two later, livestock shortage lifts, in a punishing wave, meat prices in town. If at the time when meat prices increase, there is normal weather and normal acre yields, there soon results an overplanting of grain crops, and a serious fall in grain prices. It should be remembered that the great drought of 1894 was followed by very low grain prices in 1896. Cheap grain and high-priced livestock allow unusual livestock profits for a year or two, at the end of which time former supplies are usually restored.

The 1934 drought eliminated most of the surpluses which had been accumulated in the United States from 1928 to 1933. Cotton and tobacco are the exceptions; but the 1934 adjustment programs will do a great deal to bring these towering post-war surpluses down to normal. A reduction due to drought does not mean that a lasting adjustment has been made. It means nothing permanent toward restoring a fair price, from year to year, for the product of the 370,000,000 acres of crop land which we planted during the 1920's. Given normal weather we have still every reason to believe that we have now an effective market for the product of only about 330,000,000 acres of the United States.

The drought of 1934 may seriously distort the judgment of this people as to the nature of the agricultural problem in normal years. To avoid this distortion, it seems to me especially important that we appeal to common-sense and to a long record of glut and famine, with facts. The idea of an ever-normal granary can be used not only to stabilize grain prices and supplies, but also to stabilize meat production. It is a far more hopeful concept than that of submitting dumbly to widely fluctuating supplies and to prices initiated by the unreined vagaries of nature and the distortions of speculative greed.

CHAPTER
XVIII

PUTTING OUR LANDS IN ORDER

THE Chinese are the greatest individualists on earth. They cut their forests, silted up their streams, and destroyed millions of acres of their land by erosion gullies. Thus, they became increasingly subject to flood and drought. Their soil, exposed without cover to high winds, blew around in raging dust storms. The Chinaman's individualistic treatment of the land has exposed the Chinese again and again to famine.

They have been there a long time. Destructive as they have been, we in the United States, during the past mere 150 years, have handled our land in a way that indicates even more destructive possibilities. Over large areas we are even worse than the Chinese, because we made no real effort to restore to the soil the fertility which has been removed.

We have permitted the livestock men of the West to overgraze the public domain and so expose it to wind and water erosion. Much of the grass land of the great plains has been plowed, exposed, and allowed to blow away. Timber land under private ownership has been destructively logged off, without proper provision for leaving seed trees. All of this has been careless, thoughtless, wanton and to the disadvantage of nearly every one, immediately and in the future.

Early in the century, the conscience of our people began to awaken, under the leadership of Gifford Pinchot and Theodore Roosevelt. One hundred and sixty million acres of western public land were withdrawn from entry and set aside as great national forests. Places of great scenic beauty were set aside as National Parks. More recently we have appropriated money year by year to buy new land to incorporate in the national forests.

There are now 230 million acres of land in private ownership which are in serious danger of being exploited in ways harmful to the public welfare, and which should be purchased as rapidly as possible. During the 22 years of the Weeks' Forest Purchase Act, previous to this Administration, a total of 4,700,000 acres of forest land had been acquired. During the first year and a half of this Administration, this 22-year total has been slightly exceeded, and if this rate of acquisition is continued, the forest resources of the United States will be under adequate supervision and the headquarters of streams will be protected from erosion and unduly rapid run-off within twenty years.

Under the leadership of Franklin Roosevelt, the whole land problem has received an emphasis such as it never had before. As a young man, he was a close student of the Pinchot conservation policies, and he set out thousands of trees on his own farm. As Governor of New York, he had inaugurated a policy of buying poor land and reforesting it. As President, he soon saw the foolishness of spending millions in public works money to irrigate new land while at the same time, the AAA was taking land out of use. His suggested solution was to unify the program by allocating money to buy sub-marginal land to off-set the new irrigated land. To carry out this policy, 25 million dollars were allocated by Public Works in 1934 to buy poor land.

In the meantime, as a result of the AAA taking out of use 40,000,000 acres of crop land on 3,000,000 different farms, there was growing interest in a more permanent solution. Sensible business men said, "Let's buy these surplus acres and have done with it instead of renting them year after year." Economists pointed out that it would be much sounder to take out of use the 70,000,000 poorest acres of crop land concentrated in the sub-marginal areas than 40,000,000 average acres on 3,000,000 farms scattered all over the United States. The best farmers on good land had adopted rotations and reduced their percentage of land in a cash crop like corn and cotton to 20 per cent but were getting yields twice that of their neighbors. Poor farmers on poor land without rotation sometimes had 60 per cent or more of their land in cash crops and were getting yields only half as great as their neighbors, or one-fourth as great as the good farmers. From the standpoint of pure mathematics, and of getting as much as possible out of our farm labor, it would seem that we should not take any of our good land out of use, but should confine our attention to buying poor land.

Unfortunately, from the standpoint of meeting the agricultural emergency at any time in the next five years, the proposal to buy poor land is not as practical as it sounds. In the first place, people living on the poorest land do not sell much. If we bought the 100 million poorest acres of farm land, we probably would not cut the crop output of the United States as much as 5 per cent. Moreover, the people who sell their poor land will often buy better land, and that leads to the application of more labor to the better land of the United States.

In the second place, the purchase of sub-marginal lands must of necessity be slow, partly to protect the government from the standpoint of reasonable price and good title, and partly to protect the human rights of the people living on the poor land. Franklin Roosevelt, working out the New York land problem as Governor of New York, solved the human side of the problem by giving a life estate in the property under consideration to old couples who were so fond of a particular spot that they did not want to move. Human rights must be conserved, and the government must not be cheated. Of necessity, then, the land program will develop so slowly that it will not greatly help the agricultural emergency at any time in the next five years.

Nevertheless government land purchase of poor and eroded land should be pushed with all possible speed. Human beings are ruining land, and bad land is ruining human beings, especially children. There are certain poor land regions so remote that it is impossible to maintain decent schools, roads and churches. It would be economy not to permit such areas to be settled except perhaps by childless adults who do not expect ever to lead civilized lives. Some areas are so unproductive that they will actually produce more food per acre if returned to natural game cover and restocked with wild life.

The human waste on poor land is even more appalling

than the soil waste. The Federal Emergency Relief has
approached the land problem from the standpoint of farmers now on relief. Several hundred thousand of these have
been trying to accomplish the impossible, but they didn't
know it until their endurance was sapped, and their case
made plainly hopeless by the depression. With these
families, the smaller part of the problem is buying the
miserable land where they have been trying to make a
living. The difficult thing is to find a new and better place
for them to go—a place that will not mean that the government, in placing them there, is simply subsidising
trouble for someone else. While no hard and fast rule can
be drawn, it would seem that in the eastern half of the
United States, the ideal location for many of these poor
land farmers who are now on relief would be on self-subsistence homesteads where part of the family can work in
industry. This may also be the destiny of some of the
unemployed in our cities. It costs only one-third as much
to take care of a farm family on relief as a city family, and
if the Federal Relief has to support several million families for several years, it will try to make the money go as
far as possible by getting several hundred thousand of
them out on the land, establishing them in part-time farming and part-time industry.

This trend is a matter of grave concern to established
industry and agriculture. We in the AAA will of course
insist that these government financed people do not produce farm products for sale. Industry will probably insist
that they do not produce industrial products for sale.
But industry can not solve the problem this easily, because

ultimately industry through the income tax has to foot the government relief bill.

The 10 million unemployed plus the 5 million living on land which can never be farmed are a continuing menace to the established industry and agriculture of the United States. To solve it means decentralized industrial planning relative to land. If the heads of our two hundred leading corporations were to take into account the full significance of paved roads, autos, trucks, high line electricity, and the increased happiness of human beings close to the land, might they not enthusiastically start a decentralized, industrial, self-subsistence homestead program on a scale which would jerk us out of the depression for years to come?

If industry does not seize this opportunity, its only effective defense against serious trouble will be such a revival in business that two-thirds of the unemployed will be put to work again at their accustomed places in the big cities. It would seem high time for those big industries which are truly conservative and interested in their long-time welfare to begin to do a little real planning about the unemployment problem. Agriculture should be in on this, because the wrong kind of decentralization would increase the burden of agriculture.

Land planning is no longer an academic question. A wise use of our land is intimately related to future of industry and the unemployed. So long as there are more than five million unemployed in the United States, there will be a steady and irresistible push toward the lower living costs of open country. Nearly half of the unemployed are under thirty years of age. The larger part of them have at least high school education and many have college diplomas. They are well equipped in mind and body and can see no good reason why it is so hard for them to find jobs.

As I have indicated, there is some danger that these younger unemployed, joining hands with farmers who have been in the most serious trouble, and with certain other underprivileged groups, will push the nation so far to the left that we will be headed toward the land of nightmare, even as the unemployed youths have succumbed to misguided leadership in certain foreign countries. This group, by asking more relief year after year than the Government can afford, can eventually bring on an uncontrolled inflation. To avoid this disaster, it will be necessary to get more and more of our people thinking seriously about that continuously balanced harmonious relationship which I call the Land of Tomorrow. The industries of the country must be brought definitely face to face with their responsibility for these unemployed. If they dodge, it will be the duty of the Government to go ahead with its own method of rehabilitation and build out of the unemployed a self-subsistence system of exchange cooperatives which are outside the capitalistic system.

The repeated droughts of the last five years demand special attention to another critical maladjustment. During the last 70 years several generations of suckers have been enticed by real estate men to the western great plains in years of good rainfall, only to be burned out later. This sort of robbery should not be perpetrated. No state can build a permanent prosperity on the falsehoods of realtors and promoters. Wisconsin has recognized this by adopting a zoning law which divides the state in such way as definitely limits the field of these predators. Their game can be rather definitely limited to areas where a man has at least a gambling chance to make a living at farming.

Persons deeply interested in ducks, pheasants, deer, fish and other forms of game, and who lament the passing of these native species, want the government to acquire the poorer types of land, especially low-land pastures and meadows near streams and lakes, for game refuges. By planting the right kind of shrubs and grasses and protecting nestlings from pasturing and mowing, we can work wonders in restoring wild life over considerable areas unfit to farm.

In the eastern half of the United States, we need national recreational parks fifteen or twenty miles from the larger cities. These parks might well be located where most of the land is so rough that farmers there are making a miserable living now.

Because of white encroachments, many of the Indian reservations are now terribly short of land. An increase in Indian population has contributed to this jamming-in of too many Indians on too little land. Indians are already subsistence farmers. To transfer to certain of their land-hungry tribes the sub-marginal land of the neighborhood, would seem to be both fair and wise.

Other poor land might well be turned over to the Erosion Service to see what can be done to restore it. If nothing else can be done with it, it can be put into long-time use under the Forest Service, the National Parks Service, or restored to the Public Domain.

Certain large areas of the great plains now plowed, should be put down to grass again. Some of these regrassed areas might be grazed by cattle, under controlled conditions. Other areas of regrassed land might be best restored to wild life, including antelope, deer and buffalo.

But these are fragments. Fortunately the whole land question will probably be debated at length in 1935. In June of 1934, President Roosevelt appointed a special natural resources committee—the Secretary of the Interior, Secretary of War, Secretary of Agriculture, Secretary of Labor, Frederick Delano, Wesley C. Mitchell, Charles Merriam, and Harry Hopkins.

Frederick Delano, serving as chairman of a special advisory committee of this board, has prepared a report which will be submitted to Congress when it meets in January of 1935.

When this report is submitted we shall have had the benefit of some of the preliminary experience gained by spending a part of the 25 million dollars for purchase of sub-marginal land. We shall know more definitely the nature of the obstacles and how fast we can go.

The Federal Emergency Relief Administration has been discovering more definitely the areas where the farm people have the lowest standards of living and where it is impossible, one year after another, to make enough out of the soil to raise the children decently. Already the FERA has had some experience with buying out farmers in western South Dakota, and in providing them a better farm opportunity in eastern South Dakota. The money for purchasing the land in eastern South Dakota has come in considerable measure from the Farm Credit Administration, but a part of the money has also been furnished by the FERA, on the theory that such expenditure would reduce the relief load next year, and for years to come.

In the past, our land policies have often contradicted and cancelled each other. The government had no agency to unify such policies. Both the land and its people have suffered.

This year we are really beginning to build on the foundation nobly laid by the forest acquisition policy of Theodore Roosevelt and Gifford Pinchot. The report submitted by the natural resources committee to Congress in January of 1935 will, in all probability, if the Congress and the American people are willing, furnish the blueprint for putting our lands in order. In many parts of our social structure the blueprint method of approach is not advisable, but land is so fundamental and precious a heritage, that we should outline a policy to continue over many administrations, and stick to it for the sake of our children and their great grandchildren. The alternative is to maim and misuse our basic heritage, as have the Chinese.

CHAPTER
XIX

THE COST OF CONTINUOUS BALANCE

NEW freedoms and new deals nearly always cost millions of dollars. But the greatest cost is the social discipline required to bring new ways of looking at things. To pay the financial cost of a new deal is tremendously serious; but the pain involved in changing minds and ways is even greater.

We are free, as I have said, to travel from place to place as we choose, swiftly and comfortably in our automobiles, but we pay for this freedom by submitting to the red and green traffic lights which tell us when to stop and when to go. Social discipline in the United States makes the rule that we drive on the right-hand side of the street, and that when we turn left, we hold out a hand. Very young automobile drivers may feel that their style is cramped by having to submit their rugged individualism to rules. Experienced drivers realize that their freedom is enhanced by the rules, and nine out of ten drivers learn to know the game. Millions of us move from place to place in our cars with a remarkable degree of freedom, when we take into account the definite physical difficulties of moving so many cars such a great distance at such a speed.

Most of us buy our licenses, abide by the traffic rules, and in other ways cheerfully pay in terms of social discipline the cost of our freedom as motorists. Our automobile rights involve automobile duties, and they are cheap at the price.

But when it comes to a situation like the American Revolution or a far-reaching new deal, it is much easier in the earlier stages to talk about the rights and forget the price that must be paid, in terms of duty and social discipline.

It was inspiring for our Revolutionary forefathers to adopt the Declaration of Independence. That document was chiefly a statement of political rights. It was much more difficult to realize those rights, first, by fighting to a successful conclusion the Revolutionary War; second, by going through the confusion of the Confederation; and third, by adopting the rules of social discipline between the States embodied in the Constitution. The American Revolution cost the Colonists a sum which in those days seemed very great, but in the long run, the true cost had to be paid by the social discipline which grew out of the rules laid down in the Constitution.

During the greater part of the 19th Century, we had no particular need either of a new declaration of rights, or of a social discipline to go with them. We were busy conquering a continent, and the essential thing was to stick together until that job was done. It was necessary to develop a special drive of social discipline during the sixties in order that we might keep our minds and wills focused on the common problem until the continent was filled up.

When everyone began to realize finally that the country was really filled up, that there were no more good homesteads and no frontiers to flee to in times of depression, there was great uneasiness. The day which we feared had come upon us. At last we had to learn to live with each other.

The problem from which our European ancestors fled was beginning to stir us. But in 1912, when Woodrow Wilson delivered his campaign speeches on the "New Freedom," the force we feared in the United States was represented by monopolies and trusts rather than by aristocracy. Woodrow Wilson's new freedom was the right to discuss in public those governmental decisions which had so long been made by government on behalf of business, by devious methods, with big corporations working through our political bosses.

Woodrow Wilson and Theodore Roosevelt believed that an inward rottenness could be cleansed by public exposure. Wilson's new freedom consisted essentially in telling the common people of the United States what was going on in private, so that they might vote intelligently. The rights expressed in the Wilsonian freedom were never crystallized into an effective social discipline. The World War came to upset the significance of all that Wilson was trying to accomplish.

The New Deal of Franklin Roosevelt expresses the rights of men somewhat as follows:

1. A job for every one who wants one.
2. Wages high enough to leave no one in serious want.
3. Hours of labor short enough to give every one time to enjoy life.

4. Adequate insurance against unemployment and old age; perhaps, also, against injury and sickness.
5. Comfortable housing at moderate cost for all.
6. Sufficient planned utilization of the land and other natural resources so that unnecessary depletion by erosion and similar processes will be avoided.
7. Maintenance of such democratic institutions as free speech, free criticism and free conscience.

In brief, the New Deal places human rights above property rights and aims to modify special privilege for the few to the extent that such modification will aid in providing economic security for the many.

Such proclamations sound exceedingly attractive, especially in time of depression. But it is much easier to phrase them than it is to bring them into practical reality. Providing for human relief in times of serious depression costs enormous sums. But it may cost even more to build a firm foundation to prevent recurring economic crises.

The monetary cost, as I have said before, is not the most important. The money can be found, provided we are willing to endure year after year the cost of the social discipline. For my part, I doubt if we can attain these social objectives year after year unless we are willing to modify our attitudes in the light of the four conditions I have discussed elsewhere in this book:

1. We are no longer a pioneer nation with free lands. We cannot, therefore, solve our depressions by pushing our unemployed out where land is cheap and labor is scarce.
2. Our whole psychology has been one of producing to the limit, and postponing our consumption until some future time. As a result of our enormous natural resources, our scientific understanding and our methods of mass pro-

duction we have been able to turn out an enormous quantity of goods per hour of man labor. But our economic machinery for distribution and consumption was always based on the theory of competitive scarcity. In brief, our economic machinery has not been able to keep pace with our mechanical machinery.

3. The United States, as a result of the World War, shifted with exceeding suddenness from a debtor to a creditor nation, which has made necessary a complete shift in her attitude toward other nations at a time when, as a result of the World War, it was impossible psychologically for us to make a sufficient shift.

4. The steadily increasing concentration of industrial activity into a few great corporations has destroyed the effectiveness of the free and open market as a device for balancing economic interests.

No great nation has ever had forced on to it the necessity for making such a terrific shift in its attitude so suddenly. From 1930 to 1933 our will and understanding were apparently paralyzed. It seemed impossible for us to act in accord with facts. It still is very difficult for us to do so. The more general rights of the New Deal are recognized as legitimate and worthy by the great majority of American people, but the duties are not widely recognized. The rights, unfortunately, cannot be indefinitely realized unless the duties are shouldered.

In our pioneer days a vigorous Protestantism did much to inculcate the necessary sense of duty. Duties were willingly borne as a means of expressing one's religious belief. Protestantism, when thoroughly believed in, makes it possible for the individual to tighten his belt, cut down his expenditures, and go on working in the hope of a brighter day to come. This belief, held by millions of our people, makes it possible to accumulate billions of dollars of capital.

Millions of fourth- and fifth-generation Protestants who no longer go to church continue to respond to the social discipline which has been handed down to them in the home. The theological significance has been largely forgot, but the children are inculcated with the idea that there is a supreme virtue in self-denial, continuous hard work, and putting by something for a rainy day.

Benjamin Franklin, Calvin Coolidge, John D. Rockefeller, and Andrew Mellon furnish admirable examples of the Protestant spirit earnestly at work in the world of affairs. Such men tend to believe that everything will eventually be lovely if the individuals in a nation practice thrift and hard work. In an economy of scarcity they may have been right, but in an economy of abundance—potential, at least, if not yet realized—other qualities and other duties are more clearly called for.

One great problem of the future is to hold over from pioneer Protestantism the emphasis on the sacredness of the individual, and at the same time to raise the general mental and emotional horizon to comprehension that we have now become a mature nation with abundant means of production. The need henceforth is not to learn how to compete with each other for enough of this world's goods, but to learn how to live with each other in abundance.

Specifically, it becomes a modern duty to make individual and group interest coincide. Complete dependence on individual self-interest, no matter how pious, is no longer enough to keep our complex modern economy running.

We cannot make individual and group interests coincide by fiat, at least not for long; and we cannot rely exclusively on good intentions. There has to be, first of all, a mechanism; and above all, there has to be a discipline sufficient to keep the mechanism in motion.

We have had a taste of what is involved in the NRA codes and in the AAA adjustment programs and marketings agreements. What has happened in the AAA adjustment programs gives me some hope that we Americans can modify individual behavior for the larger purposes of society. Let me for the moment return to the wheat adjustment program as an illustration.

When the wheat plan was formulated and announced in 1933, the thing that probably attracted the attention of the average grower was the prospect of benefit payments. The problem of the surplus, the necessity for combining in a common effort—all that seemed wrapped in vagueness; the offer of cash was clear-cut and compelling. So the first thought of many growers undoubtedly was, "Let's get all we can out of this."

When county production control associations were organized, and county and township committees selected, interest continued to center on how long it would be before the Government checks came in. That interest was soon complicated, however, by the announcement of State and county acreage allotments, and the necessity for figuring individual farm allotments. Checking back over his acreage and production during the previous three seasons, relying upon memory or figures scratched on the granary door, many a grower had a difficult job. Even a thoroughly disinterested individual would have had.

The first individual estimates, naturally, were not always made with their relationship to the county allotments firmly in mind. There were at least five factors operating to discourage accuracy. There was in the first place, the honest inability to recall accurately the production and acreage of former years. Second, in some counties, reliance upon assessors' estimates was unfortunate, for the reason that the assessors had accounted for only three-fourths of the average section of land in wheat. Third, in the newer parts of the wheat belt, government statistics were not as accurate as in the older parts. Fourth, there was the feeling that since everybody was likely to over-estimate, one might as well follow suit. By much the same reasoning, banks, in subscribing for Government bond issues, ask for two or three times as much as they expect to get. Fifth, in thousands of instances there was the pressure of a misery-ridden family, desperately needing every cent they could get hold of.

The intense light of publicity was focused on the individual estimates when they were published in the county newspapers. That issue of the paper was read from cover to cover. When Bill Jones, who estimated his past average acreage at 100 acres, saw by the paper that Jim Brown, his neighbor, estimated his at 120 acres; when Bill reckoned that Jim had no more wheat land than he did, somebody was sure to hear about it. That somebody was somebody on the county allotment committee. On an average there were 100 to 150 complaints of this sort in the big wheat-producing counties. That would involve perhaps 10 per cent of the farmers in the average county there.

The real test came, however, when it was discovered that in some counties the individual allotments added up to a total greater than that granted the county on the basis of State-Federal statistics. The first impulse of the growers was to say the Government statistics were wrong, and for two or three weeks the county allotment committees were on the spot. A series of deadlocks seemed to threaten the success of the whole plan. Officials of the Adjustment Administration decided they had better go out into the field and get at the root of the trouble. If there was overestimating by farmers and underestimating by the Government, the obvious thing was to find out how much of each there was.

Surveys of enough sample acreages to serve as a check clarified the atmosphere considerably.

The next step was to discuss the problem frankly with the growers in local meetings. If carefully checked Government statistics showed a base wheat area of 100,000 acres, while growers' estimates showed an area of 120,000 acres, it was plainly up to the growers to revise their estimates. The base figure for the county, as determined by impartial Government statistics, would be made as accurate as possible; but once that was done it was up to the growers to adjust their estimates to the Government figures.

Wheat growers in counties where this problem came to a head talked it over in meetings and back home with their neighbors. The feeling that the Government was wrong was somewhat shattered by the sample surveys, and by the reasonableness of the Federal, State, and Local administrators. The consciousness that within each county, the administration of the plan was, after all, up to the growers themselves, made them try more and more to figure their own way out of the difficulty. Aware that men who had overestimated their acreage were encroaching on the rights of their neighbors, the local committees determined to meet the issue squarely.

This they did in a variety of ways. In some counties they called the township committees in, put the township totals on the blackboard, pointed to the overrun in the estimates, and asked for volunteers to bring forth revised estimates. In some cases township allotments were made. In an eastern Montana County another criterion was chosen. There the producers pointed out that for years the state college had been saying, as a result of its researches, that the average farm in that region ought to have about 65 per cent of its crop land in wheat. Why not use that as a guide in revising the individual estimates? The committee agreed it was sensible, so that the growers who showed less than 65 per cent of their crop land in wheat were permitted to increase their wheat acreage estimates, while those with more than 65 per cent were asked to reduce theirs.

This democratic process of economic rearrangement went on in hundreds of counties and involved hundreds of thousands of farmers. There is some reason for believing that the first, all-engrossing interest in the Government checks gave way to corollary interests, directly connected with the problem of a world wheat surplus and the need of collective action. Despite an understandable concern with cash benefits, despite the conflicts and temporary ill-feeling this engendered, the conflicts were settled and the conditions of the wheat plan were met by the growers themselves. It was a thoroughly democratic process, and to all who participated there came a genuine sense of accomplishment. I believe that many of these farmers learned, perhaps for the first time, what is involved in making individual interest coincide with group interest.

The task of adjusting these allotments out in the counties could not have been done by Government agents. Yet the plan as a whole could not have been inaugurated without the use of the centralizing power of the Federal Government. The majority of wheat growers, I suspect, are now aware of this, and my hope is that they will realize how much a part of the Government they are, and how much the Government is a part of them. Certainly our greatest hopes for democracy lie in this realization.

It is not possible for three million farmers to go through such experiences, it seems to me, without a very real effect on whole communities in every corner of the nation. Not only wheat farmers, but cotton, tobacco, and corn-hog growers had their taste of this new venture in economic self-government. They met a million obstacles, but their social discipline was equal to them all. They did discover how to modify individual behavior in the common good.

These county associations, as one may realize, were not paper organizations, and their officers were anything but figureheads. In many townships there were spirited contests to elect the permanent committees and officers, and attendance ranged as high as 70 or 80 per cent of the eligible contract signers. The name of the president of the county association, I am told by a field observer, was spoken more times in a day than the name of the county treasurer was mentioned in two months. As a result, the officers had to make good or quit. One county chairman in Nebraska was recalled by the farmers. They felt he was "pushing himself too much."

Most of the officers and committeemen sensed their responsibility and rose to it. It took courage to ask their neighbors to adjust individual allotments downward, when that proved necessary, yet this was done in county after county. When Government money for administrative expenses was slow in coming, the officers signed personal notes at local banks to tide their associations over. Many of them, though paid a modest "per diem" when on duty, actually lost money because they were unable to look after their own farm work properly.

American farmers do not make sacrifices of time and money and personal comfort unless in response to a strong inner compulsion. As an Indiana county agent said, "If this were a bureaucratic program imposed on the farmers from above, the Government could not hire people to work the way these men are working." The agricultural editor of an Iowa newspaper put it this way: "I have found business men in Iowa who think the adjustment program came from Washington. But the farmers themselves think of this as their program. God help us when they get out of this idea. You can't shove anything down an Iowa farmer's throat—not this generation anyway. The minute anything like that is tried, he backfires. He is a peculiar individual. If he likes you, he likes you all over. If he doesn't, God help you."

When candid men who have been watching these processes at work in the field talk like that, I am persuaded that something fundamental and immensely hopeful is happening. I incline to agree with the Nebraska committeeman who told one of our field men, "The farmers are getting a taste of good government, and it will be pretty hard to satisfy them with anything less." In the long run, it may turn out that the greatest benefit of the adjustment programs may be, not the price increases or the benefit checks, but the knowledge among farmers themselves that individual and group interest can be made to coincide, and that the method employed is none other than that of a working, effective democracy.

Nevertheless, it remains, at the moment, an open question as to how much of the cooperation was obtained because of the cash, and how much was obtained because of the fundamental understanding achieved. If we do not obtain that fundamental understanding in the next year, the cash will be taken away. I mean to say, I fear that Congress will strike out that part of the Agricultural Adjustment Act providing for a processing tax. Personally, I think the processing tax is exceedingly important during the next two or three years, while the farmers are perfecting their adjustment to the new relationship which a non-lending United States now has to the rest of the world. But if the farmers do not understand the fundamental purpose of the program, they will lose the cash part of it and will deserve to do so. The fundamental part of the program is not cash but the full understanding of the necessity for making readjustments to the underlying forces so that we can attain with safety those human rights we all long for.

In some nations the people attempt to obtain a new set of rights by employing dictatorships of one type or another. Unfortunately, all dictatorships must of necessity violate right No. 7 which has to do with the maintenance of the democratic institutions of free speech, free criticism, and free conscience. The disillusioned, cynical element of the old world believes that it is impossible to realize the physical objectives of a new deal without violating democratic institutions. We who are concerned with the American New Deal believe that if the people understand not only the rights but the duties that follow, it is possible to attain the rights by submitting cheerfully and willingly to a self-imposed social discipline. We can work this out together day by day as we press into the future. There can be a rebirth of genuine democracy, and there can flow from it whatever social discipline the future requires.

CHAPTER
XX

THE PROCESS OF ECONOMIC DEMOCRACY

I FIND this book, hastily dictated, copy-read, and very little edited, under pressure of many other jobs at hand, is in the nature of an introduction to another book which might be called "The Process of Economic Democracy." The New Deal is a strenuous effort to find that process. The political democracy of a hundred years ago adequately took care of the decentralized economic forces of that day. But it is not equal to the task of balancing highly centralized economic forces, democratically and intelligently, unless certain modifications are made. Under the spur of necessity we have discovered in recent years a number of constitutional methods which may serve this purpose.

In the preceding chapters I have sketched in narrative form the events that made a new search for economic democracy inevitable. Under great handicaps, the old-fashioned rules of the game are being changed, and new rules are being discovered. But in addition to new rules we need new processes or methods that make it possible for an educated democracy to handle gigantic economic forces for the common good.

The experimental approach of recent years gives us several suggestions as to new processes:

1. The County Agricultural Control Associations, with their individual contacts inside the county and their necessity for fitting their operations into the state and national picture may be said to represent a beginning of economic democracy in action. Long after the purposes of the Agricultural Adjustment Administration have changed, the members of these County Control Associations will be utilizing the methods of economic democracy to approach national agricultural problems in a broader, more understanding spirit.

2. The code authorities of the NRA when they provide for a vital, understanding participation of labor, industry and consumers with government sitting as referee can provide in due season economic democracy in industry.

3. A national economic council should endeavor to see that the decisions of the various groups—agricultural, industrial, financial, labor, consumer—are such as promote internal and external balanced movement toward higher standards.

Economic democracy should perhaps provide the checks and balances which characterize political democracy, but it must also emphasize a prompt and active appreciation of the changing economic equities. Economic democracy must be in position to resist unwise political pressure. At the same time, it must be truly responsible to and promptly sympathetic with the pressing needs of the people from whom its power arises.

As an early instance of this process unfolding, I keep coming back in my mind to the work of the county pro-

duction control associations. It may seem that I place undue emphasis on these democratic field operations, which
admittedly are as yet in the rough, formative stages of
development. But this work in thousands of our rural
townships, carried on for the most part by the farming
people themselves, is the best example I know of the new
process. It is something new under the sun, and this fact
is too little appreciated. Too much of the news about the
AAA has, it seems to me, centered, by force of habit, upon
Washington. The really significant and enduring part of
the story, I believe the future will show, is out in the
townships of the United States.

I have observed the operations of these township and
county associations at close range. I have attended some
of their meetings, have listened to farmers discussing their
production problems and have seen them making their
own decisions on matters affecting themselves. In these
contacts, I have been impressed with the businesslike way
in which these farmers have gone ahead. The fact that the
work they were doing had never been done before seemed
scarcely to occur to them, so intent were they upon the
task itself.

One who did not know farmers might have been amazed
at the high degree of intelligence and ability shown in
these production control association meetings. From a
casual observation of corporation directors, I would say
that the average level of intelligence of the farmer com-
mittee-men as displayed in their own country meetings is at
least as high as that of the directors of the one hundred
largest corporations of the United States. Not only have
the farmers shown ability to master the problems of production adjustment, but they have proved that they can

survey the world situation and make their decisions on the basis of long-time as well as immediate factors. And the give-and-take spirit they have shown in working out their own plans, has extended and developed into greater willingness to be fair with the other great population groups.

The effectiveness of the farmers in operating these new instruments of economic democracy is of far-reaching significance. Primarily it is of significance to the farmers themselves because it shows that they do not need to suffer, helpless and supine, in the face of economic forces which they had been led to believe were beyond their control. The example may well be an inspiration to the non-agricultural groups which have been ravaged by uncontrolled economic forces.

These production control associations now number close to 4,000. They include in their membership three million farmers who have voluntarily signed contracts to adjust production of wheat, cotton, corn and hogs or tobacco.

The fact that the big adjustment programs rested upon voluntary participation of the farmers, and were carried out through the agency of the local control associations assured their democratic character. Before any of the programs were finally launched, the farmers were consulted as to the main outlines. Changes were made to suit local variations. Thus strong farmer support was assured before the adjustment contracts were drawn. In the sign-up which followed, the individual farmers signified their approval of the plans which had been drawn.

In the beginning, when the adjustment program was launched, it was not easy to get at farm opinion. But later, when the production control associations had been organized, the problem of ascertaining the farmers' wishes was greatly simplified. The emphasis placed by Chester C. Davis, Administrator of the AAA, upon the best possible census of farm opinion has been one of the strong points of his Administration. The same democratic method also stood out boldly in the preliminary planning of M. L. Wilson, who now is Assistant Secretary of Agriculture. The AAA has now so far prepared its machinery for sounding farm opinion, that we can conduct actual referenda of farmers on succeeding phases of agricultural adjustment.

In the long view of history, things that are happening now on the six million farms of the country may be the beginning of a new epoch, in which Democracy, embracing the economic as well as the political field, becomes for the first time a reality.

We can, if we choose, look backward with longing to the old kind of liberty, which was more often license for the few and economic serfdom for many. For my part, I prefer to look forward to the full realization of the kind of government of the people for which Lincoln lived and died.

In both the 5th and the 14th Amendments to the Constitution, this concept is advanced: ". . . No person shall be . . . deprived of life, liberty or property without due process of law." The 5th Amendment is part of the Bill of Rights; the 14th, applying to states, was adopted after the Civil War. Defenders of the old order now cry forth this wording in defense of their "property." It seems to me necessary to redefine the term. Obviously, "property" now does not mean what it did in the time of the founding fathers. In those days of small farms, factories and businesses, "property" had a far more tangible and visible meaning that it has now. Now, with great corporations, their shares widely held, with devices which render the shareholder's vote in fact useless to him, property is evidenced by pieces of paper. These intangible shares are not really property, in the old sense, because the persons holding them have no real control over the corporations. A man who owns a house or a barn or a piece of land can do what he likes with that property. A man with ten shares of stock in a billion dollar corporation has no more influence in deciding what that corporation will do than the most ragged vagrant in a breadline. It was on this old kind of "property," when a man had both control and ownership, that our whole theory of private enterprise, now sadly shaken, was built. The modern corporation, with its vast anonymous powers, has cracked this theory from stem to stern. We need now to redefine property rights in a way that will fairly meet the realities of today.

At the moment, it is impossible to forecast with any certainty the exact processes of economic democracy. In this book I have spread out some of the background, as I have seen it and as I have meditated upon it. I have done so in the hope that if I could tell the story simply enough it would stimulate the effective thought of some thousands of people, here and there, who some day soon will assume the responsibility for many phases of economic democracy.

CHAPTER
XXI

BEYOND THE FRONTIER

WHEN those forty thousand undisciplined slaves, the Children of Israel, left Egypt, it was possible for them to reach their promised land within a few months. But they were not fit to march a straight course, enter and take possession. The older men and women among them thought of everything in terms of the fleshpots of Egypt. Before the promised land could be attained it was necessary for the younger generation, hardened by travels in the wilderness, to come to maturity.

We have been forced away from the fleshpots. When our stock market crashed in 1929 it was plain that we would have to abandon them. We, too, know something about a new land and how it may be reached, but we are not yet fit to go in and take possession. Too many of us would like one last round with those fleshpots and golden calves. It may be that many of our younger people have been sufficiently hardened by suffering in our economic wilderness. But all will have to come to a more effective maturity before the new land can be fully possessed. Advance guards sent out to estimate the cost of the march tell us that there are giants in the way.

I am sometimes accused of undue idealism; but I know very well that it will not do to hope too much of the generation of which I am a part. It is simply impossible for us to let go overnight of the habits and beliefs of a lifetime. Younger people, if they will, can easily accomplish changes which seem impossible to older people.

Unfortunately, many of the oncoming generation now in our schools, or idling in our homes, are handicapped by an inheritance of past concepts, bitterly complicated by the present stalemate. They are stirred into potentially menacing forms of protest by the fact that the present world does not seem to want their services. If misled by demagogues and half-baked educators, they may be inclined to assume more and more that the world owes them not only a living but a limousine. Their restlessness and present disillusionment can be fatal or infinitely constructive, depending upon which side they wake up on.

After all, we middle-aged, middle-course, people have some hard thinking and many hard jobs to do, before we can reasonably expect to arouse our young to hope for an enduring democracy. Talk alone will not lead them to consolidate the position we now strive to hold, and push forward to something better.

The Children of Israel's problems did not come to an end after they had crossed the borders, or even after they had taken possession of their promised land. Their real troubles as a people had then only begun. They had put behind them a vague, nomadic wandering, but they still had to adapt themselves in some measure to the commercial features of the Canaanite civilization. Their old frontier was gone. They had to work on new frontiers. These problems, in many respects strikingly modern, provoked the strife and turmoil which resulted in the tremendous literature of the prophets and the historical records contained in Chronicles and Kings. Amos, that farmer prophet of the hill country of Judah, first raised in dramatic form the problem of social justice, fair treatment of debtors, and balanced prices.

Physically, and in other ways also, the basic structure of our land of yesterday had been torn to pieces. By the raw pioneer rules of first stakes we have encamped as migrants and have taken greedily and unevenly of its wealth. A few of us, in consequence, have much more than we can comfortably or decently spend or handle; yet most of us have too little for comfort, decency and hope of a general progress.

We face, moreover, these hard facts: First, the land frontier of the United States is gone. Depression can no longer be solved by shipping the unemployed West. We must learn to live with each other. We have no longer enormous, unexploited natural resources awaiting only the touch of young and vigorous hands to be transformed into fabulous, individual wealth.

Second, the wealth that may be drawn by the shrewdest of a rapidly expanding population is now drawing to an end. In the old days, expanding population, and the million or so of people we received annually from Europe, enlarged certain of our cities so rapidly that tremendous real estate values were reared. Today, immigration is mostly shut out. Our birth rate is decreasing. It appears that by 1950 our population will probably reach its peak, around a hundred and fifty million people, and then start declining. Our rural areas, especially in the south, furnish most of the present population increase. Most of our cities are growing only insofar as they suck in the surplus population from farms and small towns; and this surplus is falling off.

Third, enormous decentralizing forces are beginning to influence the psychology and eventually the location of many of our city families. Hard roads, trucks, autos, high-line electricity and the increasing love of city people for good air, sunshine, trees and natural surroundings, will inevitably result in drawing millions of Americans back into the open.

As we dimly discern these forces which will be at work among us for years to come, we wonder just what, in the new combination, will give to the new life the same unity that our old life obtained, simply as a result of fears and hopes centering in the frontier.

The old frontier was real. There were Indians and fear of foreign conquest. People in the older Colonies or States had to stand together against actual perils on the edge of a new civilization.

Their determination to stand together was continually renewed by romantic tales of many unknown kinds of wealth out on the frontier, of precious metals, and fertile valleys, although as a matter of fact, the old frontier was all too often a place of ragged, barbed-wire fences, dusty roads, unpainted shacks. Nevertheless, the hopes and fears that existed in the old frontier furnished a unity to our national life. For a hundred and fifty years we felt it was manifest destiny to push onward, until the Pacific Coast was reached, until all the fertile lands between had been plowed and bound together by railroads and paved high-ways.

The obvious physical task to which we set ourselves has been accomplished; and in so doing, we have destroyed in large measure the thing which gave us hope and unity as a people.

We now demand a new unity, a new hope. There are many spiritual and mental frontiers yet to be conquered, but they lead in many different directions and our hearts have not yet fully warmed to any one of them. They do not point in an obvious single direction as did that downright physical challenge which, for so many generations, existed on the Western edge of our life. Now we have come to the time when we must search our souls and the relationship of our souls and bodies to those of other human beings.

Can we build up a unified, national cultural life, unique, outstanding, one that will reinforce the cultural life of the entire world? Can we leave something that contributes toward giving life meaning, joy and beauty for generations to come?

During the sixteenth, seventeenth, eighteenth and nine-teenth centuries, ideas took possession of our fathers and grandfathers which made them resolute hard workers, men of iron, equally good as Indian fighters, pioneer farmers, and captains of industry. They suffered and forged ahead in the world, believing that there was something propheti-cally worthy in all they did. Progress Westward, land-ward, and wealth-ward was their continual urge. They exploited not only natural resources but the generations which came after. We glorify these men, grabbers and exploiters that they were, and marvel at their conquests. But they did not know how to live with each other and they did not know how to teach the American nation to live with other nations.

The keynote of the new frontier is cooperation just as that of the old frontier was individualistic competition. The mechanism of progress of the new frontier is social invention, whereas that of the old frontier was mechanical invention and the competitive seizure of opportunities for wealth. Power and wealth were worshiped in the old days. Beauty and justice and joy of spirit must be worshiped in the new.

Many of the most lively, intimate expressions of spirit spring from the joyous, continuous contact of human beings with a particular locality. They feel the age-long spirit of this valley or that hill each with its trees and rocks and special tricks of weather, as the seasons unfold in their endless charm. If life can be made secure in each community and if the rewards of the different communities are distributed justly, there will flower in every community not only those who attain joy in daily, productive work well done; but also those who paint and sing and tell stories with the flavor peculiar to their own valley, well-loved hill, or broad prairie. And so we think of cooperative communities not merely in a competent commercial sense but also from the standpoint of people who are helping unfold each other's lives in terms of the physical locality and tradition of which they are a part.

In this way, every community can become something distinctly precious in its own right. Children will not try to escape as they grow up. They will look ahead to the possibility of enriching the traditions of their ancestors.

They will feel it is a privilege to learn to live with the soil and the neighbors of their fathers. Such communities will be strung like many-colored beads on the thread of the nation and the varied strings of beads will be the glory of the world.

The pettiness of small communities will disappear as their economic disadvantages disappear. The people of small communities, rid of the pettiness which grows of economic fear, will be free to realize that community success may be truly measured only in terms of contribution to a spirit of world unity, even though political and economic ties may be very loose.

In the old days, we could not trust ourselves with joy and beauty because they ran counter to our competitive search for wealth and power. Men of the old days, whether Protestant or Catholic, accepted implicitly the discipline of the Protestant Ethic (see Weber's *The Protestant Ethic and the Spirit of Capitalism*). The men of the new day must have their social discipline comparable in its power with that of the inner drive toward the hard-working, competitive frugality of the old frontier. People may actually work harder than they did on the old frontier, but their motive will be different. They may make and use more mechanical inventions. They may do more to increase the wealth-producing power of the race.

But their efforts will, of necessity, be continually moved by the spirit of cooperative achievement. They will devise ways in which the monetary mechanism can be modified to distribute the rewards of labor more uniformly. They will work with disinterested spirit to modify the governmental and political machinery so that there is a balanced relationship between prices, an even flow of employment, and a far-wider possibility of social justice and social charity.

So enlisted, men may rightfully feel that they are serving a function as high as that of any minister of the Gospel. They will not be Socialists, Communists or Fascists, but plain men trying to gain by democratic methods the professed objectives of the Communists, Socialists and Fascists: security, peace, and the good life for all.

In their efforts they will not allow their work to be divided or embittered by the dogma or prejudice of any narrow, superficially logical, political or religious sect.

Some will seek for the fountains of an abundant life in renewed artistic, religious, and scientific inspiration. They will not, I trust, accept the animal view of human nature, put forth by the biologists and the economists of the 19th century. Of necessity, they will recognize competitive individualists and competitive nations and deal with them, as the anachronisms they are, treating them kindly, firmly, and carefully.

But the new frontiersman will be continually seeking for his fellows those satisfactions which are mutually enriching. The nature of these satisfactions can only be faintly shadowed now. They exist in a land as strange and far as was America in 1491. In this land of ageless desire we are all striving newcomers. It is not a mushy, sentimental frontier, but one of hard realities, requiring individual and social discipline beyond that of the old frontiers. It lies within us and all about us. A great seer of the human heart who lived nineteen hundred years ago called it the Kingdom of Heaven. He knew that the tiny spark of divine spirit found in each individual could be fanned into an all-consuming flame, an intense passion for fair play, man to man, and man to woman, in the little time that we are here. In the Sermon on the Mount, He spoke of the rules of the Kingdom of Heaven.

The land beyond the new frontier will be conquered by the continuous social inventions of men whose hearts are free from bitterness, prejudice, hatred, greed and fear; by men whose hearts are aflame with the extraordinary beauty of the scientific, artistic and spiritual wealth now before us, if only we reach out confidently, together.

Frontier free-booter democracy of the purely individualistic type is definitely gone unless civilization lapses back into the Dark Ages and starts over again. To maintain the good points of the old individualism and the old democracy, and yet to enable modern methods to operate over an entire continent, without injury to the rest of the world, is a challenge to our utmost sympathetic ingenuity.

At this point all of the great leaders of the past have failed. The world has never been ripe for a general success. But today our scientific understanding, our mechanical inventive power, our widespread methods of transportation and communication make possible fulfillment of the individual in the unity of the whole.

Hitherto, such talk would have been mere words and empty ideas. No one of us yet thinks clearly in this field. But millions of the unemployed, and hard-pressed farmers, as they look at the tragic waste of empty factories and idle resources, are groping in a new direction. The good things of the past, including the finer traits of rugged individualism, can make their contribution to the triumph of social, cooperative ideals, over competitive bitterness.

This means hard, definite, precise work. There may even be an Armageddon such as Theodore Roosevelt spoke of as he searched the Scripture and felt his way toward the dawn of this day.

But even though there may be grievous work, careful study, and hard fighting, the essential thing is that our spirits be continually renewed by the vision of the ageless operations that bind all humanity together. In the final analysis, our nation must serve itself by serving the world, just as you and I in serving ourselves must keep steadily in mind the needs of this nation.

These are some of the general considerations that occur as we try to peer beyond new frontiers. Because they are general in nature, they may seem to involve too exclusively a reliance upon good intentions; and to provide too little of a concrete pattern for a better order.

Good intentions are not enough,—not even good intentions backed by enlightened realization of need for less selfishness and more coordination of effort. Good intentions always have characterized human kind. The fact of aspiration is the one unfailing bulwark of stubborn hope that man can learn to master the world in a way that really expresses, "peace on earth, good will to men."

But there is need to express aspiration toward the ultimate in terms of today. There is need to set up such social forms as will give the human heart opportunity for translating its altruistic impulses into practical action.

Perhaps we can set up a few principles by which to judge proposals. It is essential, for example, that we come more

often and more fully to coordinate the thing that is individually wise and the thing that is socially wise. We can
examine each proposed new step on this basis.

From the standpoint of guiding principles for the future, there is a design drawn from the far past which seems
to be appropriate, because it suggests the maximum development of individual diversity within the limitations of
the whole. Medieval painters used to put it in one corner
of their work. It is the design used by Nicholas Roerich
for the Banner of Peace and incorporated in the Roerich
Pact for the protection of cultural treasures. The design
represents three spheres,—symbolic of the Trinity, within
a larger circle. The circle represents of course the idea of
unity. With its universal application it is not surprising
that this symbol has been used in all ages,—one may find
it perhaps, upon a Christ of Memling, an Ikon of St. Ser-
gius, or Tibetan Banner. This design has great depths of
meaning in this infinitely more complex world of today.
The uniqueness of each individual and each community
must be realized but always (instinctively, by the necessity of inner compulsion) with reference to the national
and world community. All individuals, classes and nations
which approach the future with beauty of spirit might
well unite their economic, social and cultural endeavors
within this imagined circle of unifying freedom.

Those who struggle beyond the new frontier will be
those who know how to obey economic traffic lights, and
drive social machines on the right-hand side of the road.
They will have a flair, an unconscious instinct akin to the
good sportmanship of the British upper class, that will lead

them to ask continually and intelligently in their business dealings: "Is it fair?"

At the moment perhaps, the development of such measures, in this new world—they have been imperfectly developed in the old world—doubtless, seems as remote as the flying life of the butterfly seems to the leaf-eating caterpillar.

A thousand years ago, the concept of a "nation" was entirely strange to most people yet two hundred years ago most people in western Europe saw the idea of a nation as something real, and they had an almost religious feeling about their own particular nation. The intense national loyalties that developed during the 16th, 17th and 18th centuries were decidedly useful from the standpoint of enabling the medieval communities to approach a larger life. National loyalties were rather simple in the days when there was little trading between the nations and when the communities within nations were largely self-sufficing.

Today we realize that greatly intensified communication, transportation and new methods of machinery have put the simple nationalism of the 18th century out of date. The new nationalism will not be a simple loyalty, but a very complex one, vigorously expressed in making an individual success in a particular community, but also realizing in the end, that all of us, regardless of race or color, must learn to live together peaceably on the face of this earth.

This requires a greatly increased number of people with a truly modern community feeling. I think that facts, not words, may make that feeling more general the world over.

In this country, the transition from the old to the new

is bringing forth a large number of young men who have this basic community feeling and who turn as naturally to the social opportunities opened up by the New Deal as do plants to the life-giving sun.

It is extremely heartening to see, as I do, here and there in private life and in Government Service, men who have definitely turned their backs on the mere accumulation of wealth for more satisfying possibilities on the new frontiers.

When this country's attention was centered upon money making, the successful were additionally rewarded by common adulation. The younger generation quite naturally sought the same cheap reward. I am sure that had their elders set them saner objectives in life, they would have pursued these ends, with as great avidity, for youth naturally follows the guiding hands of those whom it respects. While many a youth finds himself limited at the very start by the lack of industrial, commercial, agricultural and professional opportunities and by the competition of millions of unemployed, there is another type quick to see the large tasks of the future and to step forward with eager minds and hands.

For those who see now that the men who led us into chaos have nothing to give except another selfish fling and more chaos, new frontiers beckon with meaningful adventures.

In the preceding pages, I have tried to condense into broad material objectives the philosophy of the New Deal.

Putting our lands and factories in order is more than a day's job and holds many unforeseeable problems.

Putting our jobs in order and arranging our wages and

hours of labor with the object of greater joy in work, leisure and play will supply many a social engineer with his life's work.

Putting our houses in order in city and town and on the farm is a challenge to any architect's sense of beauty, of harmony between men, his shelter, his neighbors and his natural environment.

Putting our democratic, political and educational institutions in order so that the new order of the land, and factory and home is constantly brought to higher standards of creative living, calls for almost limitless wisdom.

In every one of these and other new directions, there are challenges and accomplishments far more real than those that rewarded the old pioneers who carried our civilization beyond the Alleghanies. The Indians, wild animals and disease of this new world are the forces of prejudice, fear, greed and suspicion, even now stirring and shouting.

I am convinced that the New Deal so gallantly started by President Roosevelt in March of 1933 will eventually fail unless sometime during the next four years at least five thousand communities are fundamentally permeated with the spirit of the new pioneers not only in a sentimental, but also in a hardboiled, hard-thinking way. They must not only mean well in their hearts, but they must understand with their minds, the adjustments which must be made in our agriculture, our industry and our monetary system.

They must have so sound a grasp on these fundamentals, that the old dealers, with short-sighted eyes firmly fixed on short-time profits, will not be able to distract them with continuous ballyhoo.

To build new social machinery requires economic engineers. But the world will not be safe for these engineers, and will not give them the opportunity really to subdue the social wilderness until the new pioneers have set their outposts in at least five thousand communities.

It is not yet certain whether the New Deal which started in March of 1933 will succeed. It may fade as did the Raleigh expedition. It may grow into a sound and real resettlement of this land. Franklin Roosevelt is doing his part and so are many of his lieutenants, but the issue remains to be seen.

Too many of us remain sodden with selfish, narrow concepts; too many of us want to see "normalcy" restored, in the old sense, and live again in plenty without facing facts. That cannot be. The world has changed. Such hopes must die.

We stand, for all our compelled activity, at a moment of critical pause. The Bull-Moosers of the Theodore Roosevelt fight in 1912 have aged into old grandmothers in the Republican Party. The "New Freedom" of Woodrow Wilson was lost in the war hysteria of 1917 and 1918. Neither of these movements reached even one-third of the way toward a new world. They died because the new world was not yet ready to be discovered.

But today it has to be discovered, and when it is discovered it must be held on to. The problem is largely one of spirit, but it is also one of hard facts and definite action continually accompanying an unfolding of the spirit.

Continually I think of a modern democracy as essentially a graded hierarchy of New England town meetings with responsible, democratically selected people dealing

with the hard facts of just quotas at every step. Again and
again the methods employed by the County Control Associations in the AAA seem to me to point the way. These
associations made thousands of mistakes. A few of these
mistakes were deliberate, with intent to defraud other
counties and other states. But most of them honestly developed the concept of justice for the parts, in terms of the
whole. More and more they dropped the mean, grasping
local attitude and stretched their thinking. They developed the backbone needed to resist the pressure of powerful men striving to get more than their just deserts.
Thousands of people thus began for the first time to think
in a vivid, unprejudiced way of larger relationships.

All of this is enormously significant especially if a more
definite social machinery is eventually provided to bring
about a council of agriculture, labor, industry and consumers.

Involved in all this is the idea of more and more decentralization of many economic and governmental functions, while at the same time the central government steps
in more decisively than hitherto to impose limits beyond
which the smaller units cannot go. Foolish as it may sound,
it really is essential to develop much more of both centralization and decentralization than we have today. Insofar as any particular class or community is likely to hurt
other classes or communities, it should be subject to certain restraints by the central government. Perhaps these
restraints can be mutually agreed upon by the conflicting
classes and regions, then reviewed and finally enforced by
the central government. In the early days of such a procedure the conflicting interests meeting in council may

tend to be rough and irreconcilable. But as knowledge increases and ultimate common interest becomes manifest, rules of fair play are made.

Under the Constitution, this general situation was recognized when the states were denied the power to levy tariffs against each other. The founding fathers were committed to the general principle of the maximum of local responsibility combined with adequate federal powers to prevent local powers from creating confusion through diverse tariff, monetary and other policies. This same principle as applied so sensibly in 1789 at the adoption of the Constitution needs now to be applied in view of the forces growing out of such developments as modern science, large corporations, changed methods of transportation, and international trade and credit restrictions.

In these matters the Federal Government should not merely restrict but also on occasion stimulate. The problem is to discover, in a definite, factual way, the powers which under modern conditions should be delegated to the community and those which should be held in the central authority.

In all this our agricultural experience has been illuminating because in our adjustment programs, we found it necessary to draw up certain national and even international objectives which could be defended as sensible to all fair-minded, intelligent people. To draw up this general policy after going into the various local situations, we felt to be definitely a Federal function. The assigning of local responsibilities and opportunities under such a broad policy was also chiefly a Federal duty. But the carrying out of the program in the states and counties was undoubtedly a local responsibility to be administered with the minimum of interference from Washington. True, Washington found it necessary at times to stimulate or restrain the local units in conformity with the national policy but the entire effort has been to create such feeling of community of effort from top to bottom that each local unit would carry out its responsibility with a feeling of pride in its contribution to the national and international well being.

I cannot help feeling that eventually the physical manifestation of the new frontier will consist in considerable measure of thousands of self-subsistence homestead communities properly related to decentralized industry. Out of these communities gradually developed will slowly emerge many cooperative ideas of profound significance to the New World.

In this connection I think of the 200,000 stranded American coal miners, most of whom have been forced out of the mines for good by the new technology. There they sit with their families in misery, but a few of them in West Virginia and Pennsylvania now have a new hope in their hearts. They know of the self-subsistence homesteads which the Government is starting, and some of the families have been accepted and are now paying for their little house and 5 acres at the rate of $15 to $20 a month. Many mistakes? Doubtless! Perhaps there will be a failure to get the necessary local industry to give them the necessary cash. But we can surely solve the difficulties if we go at the problem with determination. And when our minds have warmed to the job, we should be able with our superior resources, to improve the present approach. The challenge of the times is so decisively in this direction that thousands of young people may well consider self-subsistence Homestead Community work during the next twenty years. In such work, they can learn of that future when social invention will be even more important than mechanical invention.

Younger people can also get the feel of the future by working with certain branches of the government and with the enlightened corporations that are able to read the handwriting on the wall.

In the meantime, working with the capitalistic order as it has come to us out of the past, we can develop policies which will enable the representatives of agriculture, labor, industry, and consumers to meet together more effectively than in the past, and discover just formulæ for price and production policies. The government sits in either as a party to the negotiations or as a reviewer and enforcer. This mechanism for a concert of interest, skillfully worked out, should provide in considerable measure the unwritten constitution which will govern many of our most significant advances toward economic democracy.

APPENDIX

APPENDIX

THIS brief appendix contains a few of the more significant facts on recent economic trends, bearing particularly on the post-war agricultural depression. Some readers may want to peruse these charts and tables in connection with the chapter on "Twelve Long Years," for they contain illustrative material on the post-war boom and collapse, on our foreign trade, on the price maladjustments and on the interdependence of agriculture and industry. For additional factual material on the conditions which brought about the industrial collapse in the United States after 1929 and accentuated an agricultural depression existing in greater or less degree since 1921, the reader may turn to two pamphlets recently published by the U. S. Department of Agriculture entitled "Economic Trends Affecting Agriculture" and "Economic Bases for the Agricultural Adjustment Act."

POST-WAR BOOM AND COLLAPSE

Indexes of prices of industrial stocks and commodities, interest rates, and industrial production. In sharp contrast with the relatively stable course of agricultural income in the

---

The tables and charts used in this appendix are from the Bureau of Agricultural Economics, United States Department of Agriculture.

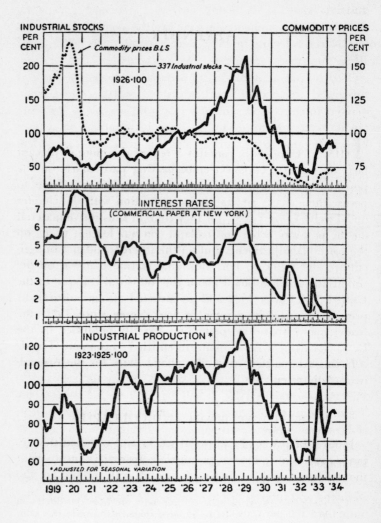

United States from 1924 to 1929 was the speculative and industrial boom. This boom, however, was not marked by sharply rising commodity prices. On the contrary, the price level, after a decline in 1920, remained relatively stable until 1929. Industries expanded their production, and the increased output at stable prices brought increased profits and supported tremendous speculation in securities. The boom derived impetus from an inflow of gold and from domestic credit expansion at declining rates of interest. As is well known, it came to an end in 1929. Among the factors prominent in the collapse were: Uncoordinated and unbalanced expansion in certain branches of industries; extreme maldistribution of the national income between city and country areas; a much greater increase in profits than in wage payments; increased competition in foreign markets, especially in agricultural products; the efforts of many countries to put their currencies back on the gold standard; and in 1929 a sharp decline in loans by the United States to foreign countries.

ELEMENTS IN NATIONAL INCOME
Agricultural, nonagricultural, and national income

Gross income of corporations that handle the bulk of the nation's business rose from $95,000,000,000 in 1921 to nearly $160,000,000,000 in 1929. It fell by 1932 to $76,000,000,000. Treating only the receipts of individuals, the National Bureau of Economic Research estimated that the national income rose near 50 per cent between 1921 and 1929 and declined from $83,000,000,000 in 1929 to $49,000,000,000 to 1932. From 1923 to 1929, the national income increased about 20 per cent. Dividend and interest disbursements by corporations increased more than 100 per cent—from $3,600,000,000 to $7,600,000,000.

| Year | Gross income of corporations [1] | Gross farm income [2] | WAGE PAY ROLLS | | | Dividend and interest payments by corporations [6] | Farm income as percentage of national income [7] |
			Factory [3]	Railroads [4]	Construction [5]		
	Million dollars	Million dollars	Million dollars	Million dollars	Million dollars	Million dollars	Per cent
1919...	...	16,935	10,462	2,828	2,250	3,189	18.5
1920...	121,600	13,566	12,608	3,682	2,250	3,415	14.9
1921...	95,300	8,927	8,202	2,765	1,990	3,342	11.0
1922...	103,000	9,944	8,648	2,641	2,810	3,400	11.1
1923...	121,400	11,041	11,009	3,004	2,980	3,585	10.8
1924...	122,200	11,337	10,172	2,826	3,330	3,841	10.8
1925...	137,900	11,968	10,730	2,861	4,320	4,086	11.1
1926...	141,100	11,480	11,095	2,946	4,360	4,391	9.6
1927...	143,200	11,616	10,849	2,910	4,480	5,571	9.5
1928...	155,900	11,741	10,902	2,827	4,520	6,028	9.3
1929...	158,600	11,918	11,621	2,896	4,200	7,588	7.8
1930...	138,300	9,414	9,518	2,551	3,720	8,600	7.6
1931...	107,000	6,911	7,256	2,095	2,760	8,226	7.1
1932...	76,000	5,143	5,022	1,513	1,640	7,006	7.0
1933...	...	6,403	5,354	1,404	1,200	6,371	...

[1] U. S. Treasury Department.
[2] U. S. Department of Agriculture.
[3] Federal Reserve Board.
[4] Interstate Commerce Commission.
[5] Estimates of U. S. Department of Agriculture.
[6] Journal of Commerce.
[7] National Bureau of Economic Research and U. S. Department of Agriculture, percentages based on estimates of farm income included in the estimates of national income, and not those shown in the table.

These disbursements continued to increase during 1930. They declined less than 20 per cent between 1930 and 1932, after 2 years of severe industrial depression. Farm income increased only 8 per cent between 1923 and 1929. It declined tremendously thereafter.

OUR FOREIGN TRADE

Exports and imports of the United States

Both the export and the import trade of the United States fell below the pre-war level in the 1931-32 season. There is a high degree of correspondence between the export and the import totals, which suggests their interdependence. Exports decline inevitably when imports decline, because imports constitute the most important means of balancing exports. In our reduced total export trade, the proportion held by agricultural commodities increased from 32 per cent in 1929 to 42 per cent in 1932-33. Nevertheless the actual volume of the agricultural export trade, as well as the value, was sharply lower.

Year beginning July	Exports			Imports		
	Total	Domestic agricultural	Percentage of total	Total	Agricultural	Percentage of total
	Million dollars	*Million dollars*	*Per cent*	*Million dollars*	*Million dollars*	*Per cent*
1909...................	1,710	871	50.9	1,557	794	51.0
1911...................	2,170	1,050	48.4	1,653	888	53.7
1913...................	2,329	1,113	47.8	1,893	1,000	52.8
1915...................	4,272	1,518	35.5	2,197	1,349	61.4
1917...................	5,838	2,280	39.1	2,945	1,826	62.0
1919...................	7,949	3,861	48.6	5,238	3,410	65.1
1921...................	3,699	1,915	51.8	2,608	1,371	52.6
1923...................	4,223	1,867	44.2	3,554	1,875	52.8
1925...................	4,653	1,891	40.7	4,464	2,529	56.7
1927...................	4,773	1,815	38.0	4,147	2,193	52.9
1928...................	5,283	1,847	35.0	4,291	2,179	50.8
1929...................	4,617	1,495	32.4	3,848	1,890	49.1
1930...................	3,031	1,038	34.2	2,432	1,163	47.8
1931...................	1,908	752	39.4	1,730	884	48.2
1932...................	1,413	588	41.6	1,168	612	52.4
1933 [1]...............	2,042	754	36.9	1,721	759	44.1

[1] Principal agricultural exports and imports only.

OUR INVESTMENTS ABROAD

New investments by Americans in foreign countries and foreign investment in the United States, 1919-32

Before the war the United States was a debtor nation. In the last 10 to 15 years, it has become the world's chief creditor nation. Foreign nations now owe us much more than we owe them, although they still have large credits here. Our balance of exports over imports prior to the war largely represented our interest payments on imported capital. In the war period foreign nations withdrew much of their capital, and we began lending to them. Our excess of exports over imports increased, but was differently balanced. It was balanced largely by our capital loans, which rose after the war to huge pro-

(In millions of dollars, i.e., 000,000 omitted)

Year	New foreign securities sold in the United States	Direct American investment abroad	Foreign and American stocks and bonds bought from foreigners	Total annual investment of American capital in foreign countries (1)	Total annual investment of foreign capital in the United States	Net amount invested abroad	Net foreign capital invested in the United States
1896-1914 ..	...	...	...	53	105	...	52
1919........	436	300	234	970	515	455	...
1920........	506	200	739	1,445	571	874	...
1921........	665	200	227	1,092	303	789	...
1922........	637	(2)	326	963	294	669	...
1923........	363	(2)	54	417	435	...	18
1924........	795	(2)	114	909	364	545	...
1925........	920	(2)	90	1,010	551	459	...
1926........	1,002	240	624	1,931	1,326	605	...
1927........	1,183	257	804	2,314	1,609	705	...
1928........	1,124	378	1,694	3,266	2,591	675	...
1929........	635	350	1,407	2,469	2,328	141	...
1930........	883	253	1,276	2,439	2,161	278	...
1931........	213	197	842	1,302	1,520	...	218
1932........	27	38	530	645	862	...	217
1933........	10	91	1,265	1,456	1,505	...	49

[1] Total for 1926-32 includes bond redemption and sinking fund payments and receipts.
[2] Not estimated.

portions. New foreign security flotations in the United States in 1928 exceeded $1,100,000,000, as compared with $363,-000,000 in 1923. But the movement of capital was not exclusively a one-way traffic. Foreigners not only borrowed; they invested large sums in the United States. In 1932 the inflow of capital exceeded the outflow. However, the United States still remains heavily the world's creditor; and this fact has an important bearing on our foreign trade, in that it compels foreign nations to restrict their purchases here.

THE BALANCE OF TRADE

The pre-war and post-war balances of international payments of the United States

(In millions of dollars, i.e., 000,000 omitted)

Item	1896-1914	1925-29	1932	1933
Merchandise trade	+488	+724	+289	+225
Shipping and freight services	—64	—56	—45	—16
Tourist expenditures	—170	—555	—375	—221
Immigrant remittances	—150	—284	—163	—132
Interest and dividends	—160	+488	+393	+389
War-debt receipts				
Government transactions	.....	+127	+32	—35
Other items				
Balance on current account	—56	+444	+131	+210
Gold and currency	—9	+25	—91	+83
Investments	+52	—517	+217	+49
Trade-credit accommodations	.....	+184	—409	—385
Balance on capital account	+43	—308	—283	—253

In the 20 years before the war we exported more commodities than we imported. In payment for our net exports, foreign countries were able to use our payments to them in the form of tourist expenditures, immigrant remittances, and interest and dividend payments on foreign investments made in the United States.

During the post-war prosperity period, 1925-29, our commodity exports exceeded imports and tourist expenditures and immigrant remittances helped foreigners pay for our net exports. The huge private and public loans to foreign countries made during and after the war reversed the character of interest payments; the United States received annually nearly $500,000,000 contrasted with a net payment before the war of $160,000,000. But these interest payments were made possible largely by American purchases of foreign securities.

By 1932 the magnitude of each of the items in our balance

of international payment was greatly reduced. The small export balance was more than offset by tourist expenditures and immigrant remittances. Interest payments were met largely by the creation of open accounts or credit accommodations.

In effect our net export of goods after the war and foreign payments on war-time borrowings, were made possible by American expenditures abroad and investments in foreign securities. The great reduction in foreign lending after 1928, has been accompanied by a shrinkage in trade and a piling up of unpaid obligations to the United States.

OUR DECLINING EXPORTS

Gross income from farm production, farm value of agricultural exports, and percentage of production exported, 1919-32

Year	Gross income from farm production	Approximate farm value of exports	Farm production exported
	Million dollars	*Million dollars*	*Per cent*
1919	16,985	2,682	15.8
1920	13,566	1,745	12.9
1921	8,927	1,390	15.6
1922	9,944	1,313	13.2
1923	11,041	1,427	12.9
1924	11,337	1,828	16.1
1925	11,968	1,464	12.2
1926	11,480	1,423	12.4
1927	11,616	1,528	13.2
1928	11,741	1,485	12.2
1929	11,918	1,215	10.2
1930	9,414	709	7.5
1931	6,911	467	6.7
1932	5,143	....	[1] 6.5
1933	6,403		

[1] Estimated.

American agriculture has been developed to produce not merely for the home market but for the world market. Almost from its inception it has exported a substantial fraction of its output. When any country, from year to year, has an exportable surplus of a commodity or group of commodities, the prices realized for the export surplus determine, in a normal market, the prices obtainable for the whole supply. The table shows how the export proportion of our farm production has declined since the war. There has been no corresponding decline in our total farm production. Here in a nutshell is much of the explanation for the post-war agricultural depression. Declining exports with mounting production naturally mean mounting surpluses.

FOREIGN COMPETITION IN WHEAT

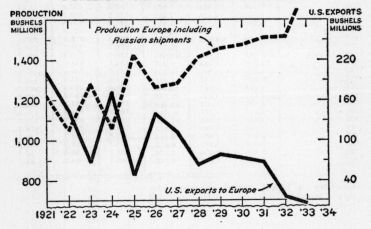

United States exports of wheat (including flour) to Europe and production in Europe, 1921-32. After the war Europe restored its wheat production. It increased the output from 1,100,000,000 bushels in 1922 to 1,500,000,000 bushels in 1932. As a result American exports of wheat to Europe declined. They were less than 10,000,000 bushels in 1933-34, as compared with 146,000,000 bushels in 1922-23.

TREND IN FARM INCOME

Gross income from farm production, United States,[1] *1909-32*

Year	Crops	Livestock and livestock products	Crops and livestock combined	Index of gross income [2]		
				Crops	Livestock	Crops and livestock
	Million dollars	*Million dollars*	*Million dollars*	*Per cent*	*Per cent*	*Per cent*
1909.............	3,314	2,925	6,238	91.6	93.0	92.3
1910.............	3,517	3,126	6,643	97.2	99.5	98.3
1911.............	3,536	2,836	6,372	97.8	90.2	94.3
1912.............	3,688	3,096	6,784	101.9	98.5	100.3
1913.............	3,647	3,328	6,975	100.8	105.9	103.2
1914.............	3,700	3,328	7,028	102.3	105.9	104.0
1915.............	3,985	3,410	7,395	110.2	108.5	109.4
1916.............	4,968	3,947	8,914	137.3	125.6	131.9
1917.............	7,431	5,401	12,832	205.4	171.8	189.8
1918.............	8,119	6,982	15,101	224.5	222.1	223.4
1919.............	9,431	7,503	16,935	260.7	238.7	250.5
1920.............	6,862	6,704	13,566	189.7	213.3	200.7
1921.............	4,488	4,440	8,927	124.1	141.3	132.1
1922.............	5,350	4,594	9,944	147.9	146.2	147.1
1923.............	5,969	5,072	11,041	165.0	161.4	163.3
1924.............	6,170	5,167	11,337	170.6	164.4	167.7
1925.............	6,147	5,820	11,968	169.9	185.2	177.0
1926.............	5,648	6,012	11,480	151.2	191.3	169.8
1927.............	5,817	5,799	11,616	160.8	184.5	171.8
1928.............	5,675	6,066	11,741	156.9	193.0	173.7
1929.............	5,421	6,497	11,918	149.9	206.7	176.3
1930.............	3,799	5,615	9,414	105.0	178.7	139.3
1931.............	2,714	4,197	6,911	75.0	133.5	102.2
1932.............	2,113	3,030	5,143	58.4	96.4	76.1
1933.............	3,029	3,085	6,403	83.7	98.2	94.7

[1] Estimates for 1929-32, revised.
[2] 1910-14=100.

VALUE OF AGRICULTURAL CAPITAL

Changes in the value of capital used in agricultural production, 1919-32 [1]

Year	Land and buildings [2]	Livestock [3]	Farm machinery [4]	Total
	Million dollars	*Million dollars*	*Million dollars*	*Million dollars*
1919...........................	54,659	8,815	3,156	66,630
1920...........................	66,316	8,525	3,595	78,436
1921...........................	61,315	6,413	3,418	71,146
1922...........................	54,190	5,104	2,728	62,022
1923...........................	52,441	5,400	2,515	60,356
1924...........................	50,476	5,117	2,651	58,244
1925...........................	49,468	5,041	2,680	57,189
1926...........................	49,113	5,403	2,739	57,255
1927...........................	47,767	5,537	2,841	56,145
1928...........................	47,670	6,041	2,850	56,561
1929...........................	47,926	6,578	3,096	57,600
1930...........................	47,880	6,490	3,302	57,672
1931...........................	43,798	4,814	3,200	51,812
1932...........................	36,851	3,500	3,000	43,351
1933...........................	30,306	2,906	2,600	35,812
1934...........................	31,655	3,072	2,300	37,027

[1] Adjusted for both changes in price level and changes in the amount of land or other commodities owned by farm operators.

[2] Based on census values of all land and buildings on census years. Values in intercensal years arrived at from index of land values per acre and adjusted for changes in acreage.

[3] Value of all livestock on farms.

[4] Value of all farm machinery, tractors, trucks, and automobiles.

DEBT AND TAX BURDENS OF FARMERS

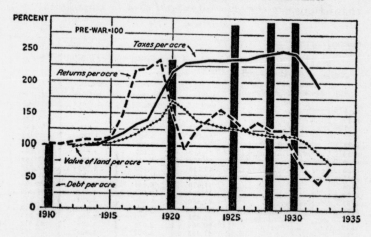

Returns per acre of ten leading crops, and taxes, land values, and mortgage debt per acre of farm real estate. Returns per acre in 1932-33 were about 60 per cent less than in the prewar years, while the average mortgage debt per acre was nearly three times and taxes about twice as high. Consequently land values for the country as a whole fell still further to about three-fourths of their pre-war value.

GAP BETWEEN FARM AND NONFARM PRICES

Index of prices received and paid by farmers. The advantage that the farmers gained during the war when prices received for farm products rose to higher levels than prices paid for industrial goods was lost in the 1920-21 depression. Relative to other prices, farm prices have been low ever since 1920, and the disparity was accentuated during 1930-32, when farm prices fell so low that they had only half their pre-war purchasing power.

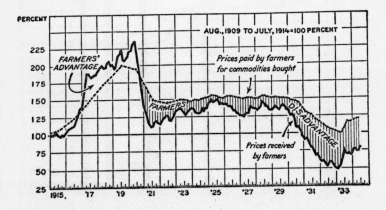

RETAIL AND FARM VALUE OF TYPICAL MONTHLY PURCHASES OF 14 FOODS PER FAMILY

The chart on page 302 illustrates how the course of a major depression affects differently the level of retail and farm prices and how the relatively smaller decline in distribution costs reduces the farmer's share of the consumer's dollar. By March, 1933, consumers were paying about $11 less, but about $8 of this came out of the farmer's share and distribution charges had been reduced only $3. This reduced the farmer's share of nearly a half of the consumer's dollar in 1929 to only about 30 per cent in March, 1933. Had the decline in retail prices been shared equally by distributors and farmers, prices at the farm in March would have been about 50 per cent higher than they were.

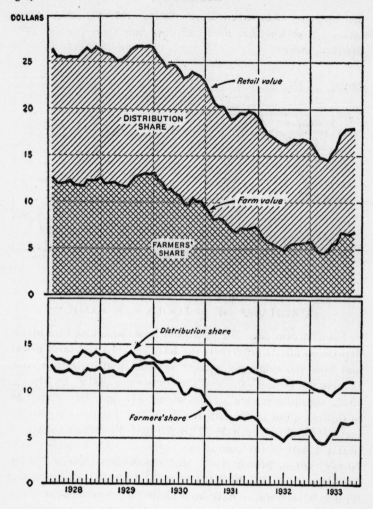

PRICE MALADJUSTMENTS

Selected indexes of prices, wages, costs of distribution, farm taxes, and mortgage interest, 1913-32

Year	Prices received by farmers	Prices paid by farmers for commodities used in—			Farm wages	Industrial wage rates[1]	Freight rates[2]	Revenue per ton-mile	Cost of distributing food[3]	Farm taxes payable	Mortgage interest payable
		Living	Production	Living and production							
1913	100	100	102	101	104	102	100	99	104	101	104
1914	102	102	99	100	101	104	100	99	105	102	107
1915	100	107	104	105	102	104	100	99	105	111	112
1916	117	124	124	124	112	108	101	97	110	117	118
1917	176	147	151	149	140	114	102	98	129	130	130
1918	200	177	174	175	176	132	130	116	159	138	149
1919	209	210	192	200	206	150	132	133	174	174	172
1920	205	222	174	194	239	192	169	144	202	211	204
1921	116	161	141	150	150	197	169	175	190	225	235
1922	123	156	139	146	146	186	158	161	175	226	238
1923	134	160	141	149	166	202	158	153	177	230	245
1924	134	159	143	150	166	218	158	153	180	230	246
1925	147	164	147	154	168	226	158	150	185	234	249
1926	136	162	146	153	171	238	158	148	192	234	247
1927	131	159	145	151	170	245	157	148	190	240	243
1928	139	160	148	153	169	245	156	148	190	241	240
1929	138	158	147	152	170	245	155	148	198	243	231
1930	117	148	140	144	152	248	153	146	196	240	221
1931	80	126	122	124	116	247	144	144	178	220	215
1932	57	108	107	107	86	216	137	143	153	191	207
1933	63	109	108	109	80	207	133	137	140	...	179

[1] Union wage rates United States as of May of each year.
[2] Average of rates on wheat, livestock, and cotton.
[3] This index represents changes in the spread between prices received by producers and retail prices for a selected group of farm products.

This table epitomises the price maladjustments that have resulted from the economic trends indicated in preceding charts and tables. The greatest degree of maladjustment occurred in 1932. Efforts have been set in motion to restore a sounder balance between agricultural prices and the prices of non-agricultural goods and services. The great problem is to make the desired readjustment permanent through a direction of production and a distribution of the income so as to meet both the demands of justice and the demands of economic stability.

THE GENERAL COMMODITY PRICE LEVEL

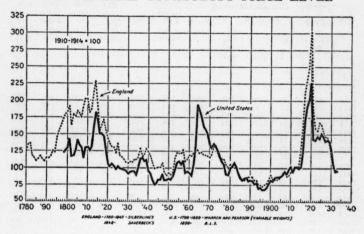

Wholesale price index numbers in England and in the United States, 1780-1932. Following the war-time rise of prices was a period of price declines broadly similar to the declines of former post-war periods. Such declines took place after 1780, 1814, and 1864. In these three former post-war periods prices returned to the respective pre-war levels, and then to still lower levels. In the 1830's there was inflation of credit and currency accompanied by land booms and by canal and railroad construction. By 1843, however, another decline had carried the general average of commodity prices to a new low point. Some credit expansion took place from 1879 to 1882.

It was associated with the resumption of specie payments by the United States Government, with active foreign demand for our surplus crops, with an influx of gold, and with industrial and railroad expansion. This period was followed by still lower levels of commodity prices in 1886 and 1896. These historical instances should not be considered as necessarily prophetic. Prices depend not merely on tangible elements in supply and demand, but on national monetary policy. The present monetary policy of the United States has features that distinguish it significantly from previous monetary policies. Usually the level of commodity prices in the United States depends to a large extent on the level of prices in other important countries. One exception occurred during the Civil War, when the United States currency prices were inflated by the issuance of greenbacks, which caused prices in the United States to rise higher than in England. Another exception occurred during 1915-20, when prices in England rose higher than in the United States, as a result of England's depreciating her currency by going off the gold standard.

POPULATION IN VARIOUS INDUSTRIES

Population of the United States gainfully occupied, 1930

(In thousands, i.e., 000 omitted)

Industry	Persons employed
Agriculture:	
Farmers	6,018
Managers	74
Farm laborers:	
Wage workers	2,727
Unpaid family workers	1,645
Others	18
Total	10,482
Forestry and fishing	270
Extraction of minerals	1,158
Manufacturing and mechanical industries	14,318
Transportation	4,439
Trade	7,537
Public service	1,058
Professional service	3,426
Domestic and personal service	4,812
Nonspecified	1,833
Grand total	48,833

With the progress of science and invention, the proportion of the population required for agricultural production declines. It now takes only about 10,000,000 persons to supply the home market and to furnish a considerable quantity of farm products for export. The United States has land and labor enough to supply all probable demands for farm products many times over. Agricultural prosperity depends absolutely on restraining production through a balanced use of these resources.

MONEY INCOME OF INDUSTRIAL WORKERS, AND FARM INCOME, 1919 TO SEPTEMBER, 1933

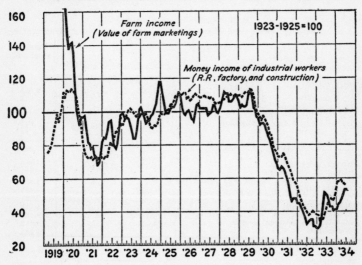

Farm income and industrial consumer incomes are basically interdependent. Some of our farm products are influenced predominantly by world conditions of supply and demand; while others are predominantly dependent upon the purchasing power in the domestic markets. By and large, however, the ultimate sources of the farmer's income is the purchasing power of consumers. At the same time, much of industrial prosperity depends upon the ability of the farm population to absorb the products of industry. In fact, at certain critical points such as at the bottom of the 1921 and 1932 depressions, an improvement in farm income gives rise to expansion in industry and consequently an increase in the purchasing power of industrial workers. Farmers, laborers and consumers have a common interest in a restoration of national purchasing power and a balanced and equitable distribution.

INDEX